تقريب التدمرية

"Towards Understanding of Tadmuriyyah"

Shaykh-Al-Islam Ibn Taymiyyah

Explained by: Shaykh Salih Uthaymeen

Author: Shaykh-Al-Islam Ibn Taymiyyah
Title of the Book: Towards Understanding of Tadmuriyyah
(تقريب التدمرية)

(First Edition/ November 2018/ Rabi Al- Awwal 1440A.H)

Translated by: Dr. Jahirul Haque(PhD Comparative Religions, IIUM)
Reviewed by: Dr. Ibrahim Ali Allafiajiy
B.A.Usul Al Deen (Islamic University, Madina)
M.A Educational Psychology, IIU, Malaysia,
PhD Educational Psychology
International Islamic University, Malaysia
Edited by : Ustaz Abu Aadil Imrann Soe Thane Z.H. Azami
Cover Design: Dr. Muhammad Alser,
M.Sc. Electrical &Electronic Engg
Universiti Teknology Petronas (UTP) Ipoh, Malaysia
PhD Electrical &Electronic Engg, Turkey
Printed at Sanatech Printings Corp., New York, USA

Published by: Daw Ma Ma Gyi Co. Ltd.
(Z&Z) Z.H.Azami & Zaybar Azami
Al-Naseehah Publications,
Kyaukse, Union of Myanmar
Tel: +95 66 50621 Email: alnaseehahpubs@gmail.com

ISBN Soft Cover: (978-1-64467-530-4)

CONTENTS

PREFACE

بِسۡمِ ٱللَّهِ ٱلرَّحۡمَٰنِ ٱلرَّحِيمِ

Shaykh Abdul Azeez Ibn Baaz, Shaykh Salih al Uthaymeen, Shaykh Bakr Abu Za'id (May Allah have Mercy upon them) and many other Scholars recommended this Book: Tadmuriyyah under Islamic Creed (Aqeedah) section to the seekers of knowledge and the Muslims in general to digest and study thoroughly. Why is it really important?

Tadmuriyyah covers the whole complete explanation of the Names and Attributes of Allah (ﷻ) and the aspects of the Divine Decree and the Legislation.

Among the creed books written by Shaykh-Al-Islam Ibn Taymiyah, Al-'Aqeedah al-Waasitiyyah (Principles of Islamic Faith), Al-Hamawiyyah already came out and printed in English by most of the publishers.

We just filled up the missing ingredient of Al-Tadmuriyyah, on your bookshelf.

May Allah (ﷻ) increase the beneficial knowledge to the humble readers.

The Executive Editor

Ustaz Abu Aadil Imrann Soe Thane ZH Azami

In the Name of Allah, the Most Merciful, the Bestower of Mercy

Introduction

All praise be to Allah(سبحانه وتعلى), we thank Him, we seek His help, forgiveness, and repent to Him. We seek refuge in Allah(سبحانه وتعلى) from the evil of ourselves and from our wicked deeds. Whoever has been guided by Allah(سبحانه وتعلى), none can misguide him, and whosoever has been misguided by Allah(سبحانه وتعلى), none can guide him. I bear witness that there is no god deserves to be worshipped but Allah Alone, and I bear witness that Muhammad is His slave and Messenger. Allah(سبحانه وتعلى) sent him with the guidance and true religion, and he has conveyed the message and fulfilled the duty, advised the Ummah, struggled in the way of Allah(سبحانه وتعلى). He left his Ummah on a clear pathway, which its night is similar to its day, none shall deviate from it except the ruined. May Allah(سبحانه وتعلى) bestow His peace and blessings upon Prophet Muhammad ﷺ, his family members, his noble companions, his rightly guided Imâms after them, and upon all those who follow them in righteousness until the Day of Resurrection.

The Prophet ﷺ has comprehensively explained to Mankind what has been revealed to them from their Lord; about their daily affairs, the minor as well as the major issues, the apparent of which as well as the hidden matters. He even taught them all they need regarding the etiquette of eating and drinking, the etiquette of relieving oneself, the etiquette of matrimony and dress, and even the etiquette of entering and leaving the house. Additionally, he taught them what they need regarding the ritual acts of devotion, such as purity, prayer, charity, fasting, Hajj, and so on.

Likewise, he taught them all they need in dealing with other human beings, such as kindness to parents, close relatives, neighbors, and so on. He taught them the system of buying and selling, the principles of lending, as well as the guidelines for business. For this reason, Abu Dharr ﷛ said, "When the Messenger of Allah left us; there was not a bird that flies in the sky except that he had given us some knowledge about it."[1]

In Sahih Muslim, Salmân ﷛ narrates that it was said to him, "Your Prophet taught you everything, even about excrement?!" He replied, "Yes, he has forbidden us from facing the Qiblah when urinating or defecating…"' – and mentioned the entire Hadith[2]. Even this was taught, so what about the fundamental basis of these acts of worship, morals, transactions; and what the slaves believe about their Lord; His names, attributes, actions, and what stems thereof – like His universal will and divine legislations that are rooted in immense wisdom and infinite mercy. The sahâbah (companions) of the Prophet ﷺ learnt all this from him ﷺ from a pure spring that was grounded in the complete Tawheed (monotheism) that stands on two major cornerstones: affirmation and negation.

Affirmation: To affirm what is befitting of

Allah(سبحانه وتعلى) in matters of Rububiyyah (Lordship), Uluhiyyah (Divinity), Asmâ' (Names), Sifât (Attributes), and actions.

Negation: To negate association of other than Allah(سبحانه وتعلى) in matters which are compulsory for Him.

---

[1] Ahmad (5/153), at-Tayalisi (479), al-Bazzâr (147), and Ibn Hibban in his Sahih (1/142, no. 65)
[2] Muslim (262)

Upon this [understanding] lived the tâbi'een (successors) who met the sahâbah, and those rightly guided Imâm(s) who came after them and still qualified for the pleasure of Allah(سبحانه وتعلى) the Mighty and Majestic,

where Allah (سبحانه وتعلى) says:

وَالسَّابِقُونَ الأَوَّلُونَ مِنَ الْمُهَاجِرِينَ وَالأَنصَارِ وَالَّذِينَ اتَّبَعُوهُم بِإِحْسَانٍ رَّضِيَ اللّهُ عَنْهُمْ وَرَضُواْ عَنْهُ وَأَعَدَّ لَهُمْ جَنَّاتٍ تَجْرِي تَحْتَهَا الأَنْهَارُ خَالِدِينَ فِيهَا أَبَدًا ذَلِكَ الْفَوْزُ الْعَظِيمُ

And the first foremost to embrace Islam of the Muhâjiruun (those who migrated from Makkah to Madinah) and the Ansâr (the citizens of Madinah who helped and gave aid to the Muhâjireen) and also those who followed them exactly (in Faith) – Allah is well-pleased with them as they are well-pleased with Him, He has prepared for them Gardens under which rivers flow (Paradise), to dwell therein forever. That is the supreme success. [at-Tawbah: 100]

After them, generations followed who were blind to the truth or ignored it, and so they were misguided and misguided others – because of either their negligence or inadvertence or transgression or infidelity. They introduced into the religion of Allah(سبحانه وتعلى) innovations in 'aqeedah (creed), 'ibâdah (worship), and sulook (character) that were not genuinely from it. They distorted the meanings of texts in the Qur'an and Sunnah, and even denied these texts whenever that was possible.

Shaykhul-Islam Ibn Taymiyah said: "Know that most of the innovations regarding sciences and worship took place in this Ummah in the later part of the righteous caliphs' era. The Prophet ﷺ foretold this, and said: **'Indeed whoever among you lives after me will see much differing, so adhere to my Sunnah and to the Sunnah of the rightly guided caliphs after me.'**"[3] Thereafter, he said: "After the caliphate ended,

[3] Ahmad (4/126,127), Abu Dawud (4607), at-Tirmidhi (2676), and Ibn Majah (42,43)

eventually leading to monarchy, shortcomings among the governors began to surface, and inevitably, shortcomings among the religious scholars had to begin surfacing as well. Consequently, the innovations of the Khawârij and Râfidah took place in the later part of Ali's caliphate, since they were related to issues of leadership, the caliphate, as the matters of legal rulings and actions that were associated with that."

The kingship of Mu'âwiyah was a kingship of mercy. However, when it ended and was followed by the reign of Yazeed, which resulted in the killing of al-Husayn in Iraq, the tribulation of the people of al-Hârrah in Madinah, which led to the siege of Makkah when 'Abdullah Ibn az-Zubayr stood up. After the death of Yazeed, the Ummah became divided; Ibn az-Zubayr was ruling Hijâz, the family of al-Hakam was ruling ash-Shâm, and al-Mukhtâr ibn Abi 'Ubayd and others pounced on Iraq – all of this during the end of the companions' era. Of those still alive were 'Abdullâh Ibn 'Abbâs, 'Abdullâh Ibn 'Umar, Jâbir bin'Abdillâh, and Abu Sa'eed al-Khudri – and they were among others who refuted the innovations of the Khawârij and Rawâfid.

At that time, the Qadariyah, like the Murjiyah, was mainly talking about the actions of slaves. These issues revolved around obedience and disobedience, believers and sinners, and so on; namely the matters of al-Asmâ', al-Ahkâm, and al-Wa'd wal-Wa'eed. They had not yet begun talking about their Lord, nor His attributes, until late in the era of the tâbi'een. By the beginning of the 3rd century after Hijrah, late into the Umayyad dynasty, most of the successors of the tâbi'een had died. Among these three centennial generations, the prominent segment from each century was the middle. Most of the sahâbah (RadiAllaho Anhom) died within the era of the four rightly guided caliphs; very few of those who attended Badr remained after that. Similarly, most of the tâbi'een died within the late era of the youngest sahâbah, during the reign of Ibn az-Zubayr and 'Abdul-Malik [ibn Marwân]. As well, most of the successors of the tâbi'een died by the end of the Umayyad dynasty and at the beginning of the Abbasid dynasty. Many non-Arabs became leaders and many books became translated into Arabic from the Persian, Indian, and Roman languages. At this time, the statement of the Prophet ﷺ became most evident: **"Lying will become widespread, until a man will give testimony without being asked to do so, and will vow without being asked to do so."**[4]

Three issues unfolded: Conjecture (Human discretion), Philosophy, and Sufism.

Likewise, at-Tajahhum; which is denying the Attributes of Allah, vis-à-vis at-Tamtheel which is similitude "making Allah similar to His servant" took place during that time...

Later, Ibn Taymiyah continued to say: "Indeed, knowing the origins and fundamentals of any matter, and knowing the religion and its origins, and the basis for whatever became introduced into it, is one of the most beneficial sciences. This is because so long as a man remains unaware of the realities behind the matters he needs, envy will forever remain in his heart as a result."[5]

Ibn al-Qayyim, may Allah(سبحانه وتعلى) bestow mercy upon him, said: "The innovation of al-Qadar took place in the late era of sahâbah, so those sahâbah who were still alive at that time, like 'Abdullâh Ibn 'Umar رضي الله عنه, Ibn 'Abbâs رضي الله عنه and others condemned it strongly. Then, the innovation of Irjâ' occurred after the era of the sahâbah had ended, so their contemporaries among the tâbi'een protested against it. After the era of tâbi'een, the innovation of at-Tajahhum surfaced. It reached full strength and became most perilous during the era of the Imâms, like

4 Ahmad (1/18,26), at-Tirmidhi (2165), and Ibn Majah (2363)
5 Majmoo' al-Fatâwâ (10/354-368)

Imâm Ahmad ibn Hanbal and those with him. Following that, the innovation of al-Hulool (pantheism) surfaced in the time of al-Husayn ibn al-Hallâj. Whenever Satan concocted these innovations or their likes,

Allah(سبحانه وتعلى) erected individuals from among His cherished slaves that would repeal it, warn the Muslims against it for the sake of Allah(سبحانه وتعلى), His Book, His Messenger ﷺ, and the people of Islam."[6]

Ibn Hajar – may Allah(سبحانه وتعلى) bestow mercy upon him – stated in his commentary on Saheeh al-Bukhâri: "among the things that surfaced are the compilation of the Hadith took place, then the Tafseer (interpretation) of the Qur'an, then the compilation of juristic issues that were based solely on conjecture, and then the compilation of the issues related to the actions of the heart.

As for the first occurrence, it was criticized by 'Umar, Abu Moosâ, and others, while the majority allowed it.

As for the second, it was criticized by a group of the tâbi'een, like ash-Sha'bi.

As for the third, it was criticized by a small group, including Imâm Ahmad, while the fourth was strongly condemned by Imâm Ahmad.

Likewise, a compilation of the origins of religions also took place, which caused two groups to come into existence: al-Muthbitah (those who approve them) and al-Nufat (those who disapprove them). The first group exaggerated until they equated Allah(سبحانه وتعلى) with His creations in some Attributes, and the second group exaggerated until they denied some of Allah(سبحانه وتعلى)'s Attributes. The criticism from

[6] See: [Tahdheeb Sunan Abi Dâwud] (7/61)

the salaf like Abu Hanifah, Abu Yoosuf, and ash-Shâfi'i rapidly became stronger, and their statements against Ahl al-Kalâm (the people of rhetoric) are well known. The reason for this dispraise was that these people talked about an issue that which the Prophet ﷺ and his companions were silent about. It is reported from Malik that these innovations, like those of the Khawârij, Rawâfid, and Qadariyyah were not in the time of the Prophet ﷺ, Abu Bakr, or 'Umar. In most cases, it only spread after the three preferred generations and was then criticized by the Imâms of tâbi'een, and their followers. The people of innovation did not stop there but rather continued to jumble the religious issues with Greek philosophy. They even put their philosophy as a standard to measure the religious issues against in case of confliction, to the extent that they would at times misinterpret them intentionally. They considered their science superior to all and would advocate its learning as the first obligation upon a person. To them, those who did not practice this philosophy were unlearned and ignoramus. In reality, the blessed people were those who adhere to the teachings of the Salaf and avoid the innovations of Khalaf (later generations). If this (philosophy/science) cannot be avoided, then one should suffice with that which serves his need, while retaining the former as his primary aim."[7]

As Allah(سبحانه وتعلى)'s wisdom dictated the existence of opposition to the truth; those whose opposition of the truth allows the truth to become clear from falsehood, for pure gold does not surface until it is put in the fire. Consequently, He appointed individuals, by His flawless Power, His Subtleness and Compassion, and His Irresistible Strength, that would refute these opponents and expose the fallacies in their arguments in accordance with saying in the poem. Baseless arguments are like remnant broken bottle indeed, every breaker will become broken.

---

[7] Fat-h al-Bâri (13/253)

Imâm Ahmad says in the preface of his book, ar-Radd 'alâ al-Jahmiyyah: "All praise be to Allah(سبحانه وتعلى), Who appoints some of the people of knowledge, at intervals between the prophets, who call misled people to the right path, and endure patiently despite the harms. They revive with the Book of Allah(سبحانه وتعلى) those that have died and illuminate with the light of Allah(سبحانه وتعلى) those that have become blind. How many victims of Iblees (Satan) have they returned to life, and how many lost and confused souls have they guided. How splendid is their effect on the people, and how awful is the effect of the people on them. They clear the Book of Allah(سبحانه وتعلى) from the distortions made by the extremists, the plagiarism of the imposters, and the wrong interpretations of the ignorant; those who raised the banners of bid'ah (heresy) and unleashed the reins of fitnah (tribulation). They differed regarding the Book, and they all opposed the Book, yet they all agree on opposing the Book. They speak against Allah(سبحانه وتعلى), and about Allah(سبحانه وتعلى), and about His book without knowledge. They speak in vague terms, by which they deceive the ignorant with such vague terms, and we seek refuge with Allah from the fitnah of the misguiders."[8]

One of those people whom Allah (سبحانه وتعلى) appointed for the support of His religion, and its defense using tongue, hand, and spear, was Shaykhul-Islam Abu al-'Abbâs Ahmad ibn 'Abd al-Haleem ibn 'Abdis-Salâm ibn Taymiyah. He was born on Monday, the 10th of Rabee'al-Awwal of 661AH, in Haran. He died while wrongfully imprisoned, in the Citadel of Damascus, on Monday night, the 20th of Dhul Qi'dah of 728AH. His funeral prayer was performed at the 'Umayyad Mosque after Dhuhr prayer. Due to the excessive crowds, it was not possible to bury him until shortly before the 'Asr prayer. May Allah(سبحانه وتعلى) bestow abundant mercy upon him and gather him and us with those whom

[8] See: [Ijtimâ' al-Juyoosh al-Islamiyah] by Ibn al-Qayyim.

Allah(سبحانه وتعلى) has honored in the gardens of bliss.

He has many writings in which he argues with the people of innovation and refuses their thoughts; of them being long, medium, and short lengthed writings. Certainly, these writings benefited the Ummah greatly, as Imâm Ibn al-Qayyim - may Allah(سبحانه وتعلى) bestow mercy upon him – indicates in his poem, an-Nuniyah poetry, wherein he says:

If you want to see their demise you will find that they are those infidel nations who suspend the name and attribute of Allah(سبحانه وتعلى).

Until he said:

Truly, read the write-ups of Imaam, the eminent, the knowledgeable and the Godly scholar.

I mean, Abu al-'Abbaas the sea, the ocean with all passions.

Also, read about his intellectual book ('Aql) and Naql (Quran /Sunnah) book, he has no comparison.

Likewise, read about his Manhaj in responding to the statement of al-Rawaafidh (a sect of Shi'ite) who are followers of Shaytaan.

Then he mentioned several of his books and letters and said:

His books are widely known by people and sold with exorbitant prices.

He has great status among people; which he established for the sake of Allah(سبحانه وتعلى) without fear.

He helps Allah(سبحانه وتعلى)'s religion, His Book and His Messenger as well, with sword and clear evidence.

He always disclosed their scandals, ignorance and contradictions

Until he said, it is amazing, that he destroyed them with the weaponry and set them low.

Our forelocks were imprisoned in their hands before, and now we are secure from them.

Their Kings become slaves and helpers of the Prophet ﷺ by the Mercy of Allah(سبحانه وتعلى).

One of Shaykhul-Islam Ibn Taymiyah's treatises was [Tahqeeq al-Ithbât lil-Asmâ' was-Sifât wa Haqeeqat al-Jam'i Bayn al-Qadar wash-Shar'], otherwise known as [at-Tadmuriyyah].

TADMURIYYAH

Obviously, the treatise contains his rejoinders on people of Tadmur, and it is the best book of his kind in terms of the minimum. For this reason, I seek Allah(سبحانه وتعلى)'s Help to compile it and make its meaning closer to the readers with increments where the need arises, omitting what needed that will not touch the actual treatise and named it "Taqreeb Tadmuriyyah" "*the Simplifying the Meaning of Tadmuriyyah* ".

I seek Allah(سبحانه وتعلى) to make this my work sincerely for Him, consonant with His Love, and benefitting His servants. He is Benevolent.

* In reality, Allah(سبحانه وتعلى)'s Names and Attributes of the book "Taqreeb Tadmuriyyah" cannot make it simple. But our beloved Shaykh Salih Uthaymeen breaks it down for the readers **"Towards Understanding of Tadmuriyyah."**

The Rationale behind Compilation of this Treatise

The author gave account on the rationale by saying:

'Having said that: I was requested by those whom I have obliged, to put in writing the summary of what they heard from me in some lectures concerning discussions about al-Tawhid, as-Sifât; Shari'ah and al-Qadar.'

Then, he gave two reasons why he is under obligation to answer them:

1) The dire need to clarify these two fundamental issues, due to the fact that these issues must cross everyone's mind making it compulsory to have clear clarification of guidance from misguidance and truth from falsehood.
2) Enormous inconsistency in people's opinions regarding the two issues. In addition, these issues are dealt with relying on the fact sometimes and on fallacy many times. This confuses many people in discerning the truth from falsehood; therefore, it should be clarified.

A Brief about Tawheed, as-Sifât, Shari'ah and al-Qadar

The issue of Tawheed and as-Sifât is a kind of information from the speaker in form of either negation or affirmation; [rhetorically information is either accepted or rejected] which must be responded to by either confirmation or rejection from the addressed. because this is information is either about what is right to be attributed to Allah(سبحانه وتعلى) such as His oneness and perfection of His attributes or that which is inappropriate to be attributed to Him, such as polytheism, the imperfection of His attributes and resemblance with the creatures.

Example of this, Allah(سبحانه وتعلى) says:

﴿ اللَّهُ لا إِلَهَ إِلَّا هُوَ الْحَيُّ الْقَيُّومُ لا تَأْخُذُهُ سِنَةٌ وَلا نَوْمٌ ﴾

"Allah; none has the right to be worshipped but He, the Ever-Living, the One Who sustains and protects all that exists. Neither slumber nor sleep overtakes Him."[9]

Here, the statement ﴿اللَّهُ لا إِلَهَ إِلَّا هُوَ﴾ indicates the affirmation of the oneness of Allah(سبحانه وتعلى), ﴿الْحَيُّ الْقَيُّومُ﴾ is the evidence of His attributes perfection. However, the statement: ﴿لا تَأْخُذُهُ سِنَةٌ وَلا نَوْمٌ ﴾indicates the negation of imperfection concerning His attributes which implies affirmation of perfection concerning the attributes.

Issues related to Shari'ah and al-Qadar

Concerning the issue of Shari'ah and al-Qadar, it is in form of demand which can be a command [to do] or prohibition [to avoid] from the speaker, corresponding to obedience or defiance from the addressed; because the request may either be about something loved by

[9] Al-Baqarah: 255

Allah (سبحانه وتعالى) and His Messenger, thus is commanded, or about something disliked by Allah (سبحانه وتعالى)and His Messenger, thus is prohibited. As Allah(سبحانه وتعلى) says:

وَاعْبُدُوا اللَّهَ وَلا تُشْرِكُوا بِهِ شَيْئاً

"Worship Allah and join none with Him in worship."[10]

Here the statement, ﴿وَاعْبُدُوا اللَّهَ﴾ is a command to worship

Allah (**سبحانه وتعلى**). The statement ﴿وَلا تُشْرِكُوا بِهِ شَيْئاً﴾ is a prohibition from associating anything with Him.

The difference between (الخبر) information and (الطلب) demand)

The difference between (الخبر) information and (الطلب) demand), with respect to their essence as well as their ruling, is well known.

As for the information relayed from Allah (سبحانه وتعالى)and His Messenger, it is mandatory for every Muslim to confirm it and believe in it according to the wish of Allah (سبحانه وتعالى) and His Messenger a confirmation devoid of any rejection, a conviction devoid of any disbelief, and certainly devoid of any doubt. As Allah(سبحانه وتعالى) says:

يَا أَيُّهَا الَّذِينَ آمَنُوا آمِنُوا بِاللَّهِ وَرَسُولِهِ وَالْكِتَابِ الَّذِي نَزَّلَ عَلَى رَسُولِهِ وَالْكِتَابِ الَّذِي أَنْزَلَ مِنْ قَبْلُ وَمَنْ يَكْفُرْ بِاللَّهِ وَمَلائِكَتِهِ وَكُتُبِهِ وَرُسُلِهِ وَالْيَوْمِ الآخِرِ فَقَدْ ضَلَّ ضَلالا بَعِيداً[11]

"O you who believe! Believe in Allah, and His Messenger (Muhammad), and the Book (the Qur'an) which He has sent down to His Messenger, and the Scripture which He sent down to those before (him), and whosoever disbelieves in Allah, His Angels, His Books, His Messengers, and the Last Day, then indeed he has strayed far away."

[10] Nisa: 36
[11] Nisa: 136

Concerning "demand" (الطلب)

It is mandatory for every human being to comply with it according to the wish of Allah (سبحانه وتعالى) and His messenger without excessiveness or negligence, so they abide by the commandment by doing what is required and refrains from what is prohibited. As Allah(سبحانه وتعلى) says:

﴿يَا أَيُّهَا الَّذِينَ آمَنُوا أَطِيعُوا اللَّهَ وَرَسُولَهُ وَلا تَوَلَّوْا عَنْهُ وَأَنْتُمْ تَسْمَعُونَ* وَلا تَكُونُوا كَالَّذِينَ قَالُوا سَمِعْنَا وَهُمْ لا يَسْمَعُونَ* إِنَّ شَرَّ الدَّوَابِّ عِنْدَ اللَّهِ الصُّمُّ الْبُكْمُ الَّذِينَ لا يَعْقِلُونَ* وَلَوْ عَلِمَ اللَّهُ فِيهِمْ خَيْراً لَأَسْمَعَهُمْ وَلَوْ أَسْمَعَهُمْ لَتَوَلَّوْا وَهُمْ مُعْرِضُونَ﴾[12]

"O you who believe! Obey Allah and His Messenger, and turn not away from him (i.e. Messenger Muhammad) while you are hearing * And be not like those who say: 'We have heard,' but they hear not * Verily! The worst of (moving) living creatures with Allah are the deaf and the dumb, those who understand not (i.e. the disbelievers) * Had Allah known of any good in them, He would indeed have made them listen, and even if He had made them listen, they would but have turned away, averse (to the truth)."

The Principle Concerning Oneness of Attributes and its Evidence

Having being certain about what has been discussed so far, two principles must be discussed here:

The first principle deals with Allah's Attributes that Allah(سبحانه وتعالى)should be described as He describes Himself and as

[12] Anfal: 20-23

described by His Messenger with an affirmation of the attributes without comparison and denial of imperfection without refutation of the attributes. As both are combined by Allah (سبحانه وتعالى) in His saying:

﴿لَيْسَ كَمِثْلِهِ شَيْءٌ وَهُوَ السَّمِيعُ الْبَصِيرُ﴾[13]

"There is nothing like unto Him, and He is the All-Hearer, the All-Seer."

The statement ﴿لَيْسَ كَمِثْلِهِ شَيْءٌ﴾ denotes negation implying perfection of His Attributes and nullification of Ahl at-Tamtheel (those who compare Allah's Attributes with that of His creatures)'s methodology.

His statement: ﴿وَهُوَ السَّمِيعُ الْبَصِيرُ﴾"and He is the All-Hearer, the All-Seer" indicates affirmation of His Names and Attributes [i.e. the Attributes of Hearing and Vision] as against the methodology of Ahl-al-Tahrif (those who distorts the words of Allah(سبحانه وتعلى)) and Ahl al-Ta'teel (those who deny the Names and Attributes of Allah(سبحانه وتعلى)). Based on this we must affirm for Allah(سبحانه وتعلى) what he has affirmed for Himself and at the same time deny what He has denied about Himself, without any Tahrif or Ta'til; and without Takyeef or Tamtheel. This is the perfect method that must be followed by all; as is the only one based on knowledge, wisdom, and accuracy in expression and conviction. It is also the only one supported by both textual and rational evidence:

Textual Evidence: As Allah(سبحانه وتعلى) says:

[13] Surah Ash-Shurah: 11

﴿وَلِلَّهِ الأَسْمَاء الْحُسْنَى فَادْعُوهُ بِهَا وَذَرُواْ الَّذِينَ يُلْحِدُونَ فِي أَسْمَآئِهِ سَيُجْزَوْنَ مَا كَانُواْ يَعْمَلُونَ﴾[14]

"And (all) the Most Beautiful Names belong to Allah, so call on Him by them, and leave the company of those who belie or deny (or utter impious speech against) His Names. They will be requited for what they used to do."

Also, Allah(سبحانه وتعلى) says:

﴿...لَيْسَ كَمِثْلِهِ شَيْءٌ وَهُوَ السَّمِيعُ الْبَصِيرُ﴾[15]

"There is nothing like unto Him, and He is the All-Hearer, the All-Seer."

Also, Allah(سبحانه وتعلى) says:

﴿فَلاَ تَضْرِبُواْ لِلّهِ الأَمْثَالَ إِنَّ اللّهَ يَعْلَمُ وَأَنتُمْ لاَ تَعْلَمُونَ﴾[16]

"So put not forward similitudes for Allah (as there is nothing similar to Him, nor He resembles anything). Truly! Allah knows and you know not."

Also, Allah(سبحانه وتعلى) says:

﴿وَلاَ تَقْفُ مَا لَيْسَ لَكَ بِهِ عِلْمٌ إِنَّ السَّمْعَ وَالْبَصَرَ وَالْفُؤَادَ كُلُّ أُوْلَئِكَ كَانَ عَنْهُ مَسْؤُولاً﴾[17]

"And follow not (O man i.e., say not, or do not or witness not, etc.) that of which you have no knowledge (e.g. one's saying: 'I have seen,' while in fact he has not seen, or 'I have heard,' while he has not heard). Verily! The hearing, and the sight, and the heart, of each of those you will be questioned (by Allah)."

---

[14] Al-A'raf: 180
[15] Al-Shura:11
[16] Al-Nahl:74
[17] Al-Isra': 36

Rational Evidence

Since knowledge about the Names and Attributes of Allah(سبحانه وتعالى)is purely based on information, which is intellectually impossible to grasp in details, it becomes imperative to restrict oneself to the textual evidence.

Integration between Affirmation and Negation

Nature of the Affirmed Attributes

You should know that all of the Affirmed Attributes used by Allah (سبحانه وتعالى) as **Integration of Affirmation with Negation.**

The combination between affirmation and negation in dealing with the issue of Attributes is the essence of al-Tawheed concerning the issue.

The root-verb of al-Tawheed is وحَّدَ يُوَحِّدُand therefore, it is not possible to attain true Tawheed without both affirmation and negation; this is because pure negation will lead to al-Ta'teel (outright denial) while pure affirmation does not guarantee exclusion. This can be demonstrated as follows:

1) If you say: Zaid is not brave, [by that] you have only denied Zaid of bravery, but if you say: Zaid is brave; you are affirming the characteristic of bravery about Zaid. However, this statement does not exclude others from also being brave.

2) If you say: There is no brave other than Zaid; you are affirming the characteristic of bravery for Zaid, at the same time, you are also excluding others from sharing with him this characteristic. Therefore, you have declared him as a unique individual with respect to this trait of bravery. In that case, it is not possible to make someone unique without integrating affirmation with negation.

Nature of the Affirmed Attributes

You should know that all of the Affirmed Attributes used by Allah (سبحانه وتعالى) as attributes for Himself are Attributes of perfection and they are generally stated in details. This is premised on the fact that the more these attributes are mentioned and indicate varieties of meanings the more the perfection of its bearer become more evident, That may be the reason why the Affirmed Attributes used by Allah for Himself far exceeded the negated attributes that Allah (سبحانه وتعالى)has negated about Himself.

Nature of the Negated Attributes

All of the negated attributes that Allah(سبحانه وتعالى) has negated about Himself are attributes of imperfection and are not appropriate for Him, such as incapability, tiredness, injustice, and similitude to His creatures, and are generally stated in brief, as that is more indicative to glorify the bearer and more perfect in ensuring His exclusion [from all shortcomings].

The Implication of stating negated attributes in details

Indeed, to unnecessarily state these attributes [negated attributes] in details, amounts to mockery and ridicule of the bearer. For example, if you praise a king by saying: You are generous, expert, hero, strong in leadership, conqueror of your enemies, in addition to other praiseworthy qualities, such would be of the greatest forms of praise for him because it includes extensive praise and detailed descriptions of his good qualities, which thus makes him loved and respected. This is because of your extensive and detailed affirmation. On the other hand, if you say: you are a king that no other contemporary king can compare to you. This will be of the best forms of praise, because of your generalizing and abridging in negation.

Moreover, if you say: You are neither a stingy king, nor a coward, nor a pauper, nor a grocer, nor a garbage collector, nor a farrier, nor a copper and the like. Extensive negation all deficiencies, which are not proper for him is nothing but a form of mockery and ridicule of his position.

Stating affirmed Names and Attributes of Allah (سبحانه وتعالى) in brief

Sometimes, the affirmed Names and Attributes of Allah (سبحانه وتعالى) may be stated in brief; Allah(سبحانه وتعالى)says regarding His Names:

﴿وَلِلَّهِ الأَسْمَاء الْحُسْنَى فَادْعُوهُ بِهَا﴾[18]

[18] Al-A'raf: 180

"And (all) the Most Beautiful Names belong to Allah, so call on Him by them."

Allah (سبحانه وتعالى)says regarding His Attributes:

﴿وَلِلَّهِ الْمَثَلُ الأَعْلَىَ﴾[19]

"And for Allah is the highest description." Meaning, the highest character.

Stating negated attributes in details

Sometimes Allah(سبحانه وتعالى)describes the negated attributes in details due to the following reasons :

1. To counter [specific] claims perpetrated against Him by liars and fabricators. As Allah(سبحانه وتعلى) says:

﴿مَا اتَّخَذَ اللَّهُ مِن وَلَدٍ وَمَا كَانَ مَعَهُ مِنْ إِلَهٍ﴾[20]

"No son (or offspring or children) did Allah beget, nor is there any ilah (god) along with Him."

2. To refute insinuation of imperfection about Allahسبحانه وتعالى) as Allah(سبحانه وتعلى) says:

﴿ وَلَقَدْ خَلَقْنَا السَّمَاوَاتِ وَالأَرْضَ وَمَا بَيْنَهُمَا فِي سِتَّةِ أَيَّامٍ وَمَا مَسَّنَا مِن لُّغُوبٍ﴾[21]

"And indeed We created the heavens and the earth and all between them in six Days and nothing of fatigue touched Us."

[19] Al-Nahl:60
[20] Al-Mu'minun: 91
[21] Al-Qaf: 38

Examples of Extensive Affirmation and Brief Negation

There are many examples of extensive affirmation; some of these are as follows:

Allah(سبحانه وتعلى) says in Surah al-Hashr, verse 22-24:

﴿هُوَ اللَّهُ الَّذِي لا إِلَهَ إِلاَّ هُوَ عَالِمُ الْغَيْبِ وَالشَّهَادَةِ ...﴾[22]

"He is Allah, than Whom there is Lâ ilâha illâ Huwa (none has the right to be worshipped but He) the All-Knower of the unseen and the seen (open)", until the end of the Surah.

These verses contain more than fifteen Names, and each name entails one, two or more attributes.

Also, Allah(سبحانه وتعلى) says in Surah al-Hajj, verse 59-65:

﴿لَيُدْخِلَنَّهُم مُّدْخَلا يَرْضَوْنَهُ وَإِنَّ اللَّهَ لَعَلِيمٌ حَلِيمٌ﴾[23]

"Truly, He will make them enter an entrance with which they shall be well-pleased, and verily, Allah indeed is All-Knowing, Most Forbearing."

Until the verse:

﴿...إِنَّ اللَّهَ بِالنَّاسِ لَرَؤُوفٌ رَّحِيمٌ﴾[24]

"Verily, Allah is, for mankind, full of Kindness, Most Merciful."

These are seven consecutive verses, every one of them ends with two of Allah(سبحانه وتعلى)'s Names, and each name entails one, two or more attributes.

---

[22] Al-Hashr: 22
[23] Al-Hajj: 59
[24] Al-Hajj: 65

The examples of brief negation are as follows:

Allah(سبحانه وتعلى) says:

﴿...لَيْسَ كَمِثْلِهِ شَيْءٌ﴾[25]

"There is nothing like unto Him."

And Allah(سبحانه وتعلى) says:

﴿...هَلْ تَعْلَمُ لَهُ سَمِيًّا﴾[26]

"Do you know of any who is similar to Him?"

And Allah(سبحانه وتعلى) says:

﴿وَلَمْ يَكُن لَّهُ كُفُوًا أَحَدٌ﴾[27]

"And there is none co-equal or comparable unto Him."

[25] Al-Shura: 11
[26] Al-Maryam: 65
[27] Al-Ikhlas: 4

The similarity in Names and Attributes

You should know that Similarity in names and attributes [between two things] does not necessarily denote similarity of those similarly named or similarly described; as this has been proven by textual, logical and sensible evidence.

Textual Evidence:

Allah(سبحانه وتعلى) says about Himself:

﴿إِنَّ اللَّهَ نِعِمَّا يَعِظُكُم بِهِ إِنَّ اللَّهَ كَانَ سَمِيعًا بَصِيرًا﴾[28]

"Verily, how excellent is the teaching which He (Allah) gives you! Truly, Allah is Ever All-Hearer, All-Seer."

About human being, He(سبحانه وتعلى) says:

﴿إِنَّا خَلَقْنَا الإِنسَانَ مِن نُّطْفَةٍ أَمْشَاجٍ نَّبْتَلِيهِ فَجَعَلْنَاهُ سَمِيعًا بَصِيرًا﴾[29]

"Verily, We have created man from Nutfah (drops) of mixed semen (sexual discharge of man and woman), in order to try him: so We made him hearer and seer."

To refute insinuation that The Hearer (Allah) is like the hearer (human being) and that The Seer (Allah) is like the seer (human being), Allah (سبحانه وتعالى) says:

﴿لَيْسَ كَمِثْلِهِ شَيْءٌ وَهُوَ السَّمِيعُ الْبَصِيرُ﴾[30]

"There is nothing like unto Him, and He is the All-Hearer, the All-Seer."

---

[28] Al-Nisa: 58
[29] Al-Insan: 2
[30] Al-Shura: 11

He(سبحانه وتعلى) affirms the characteristic of knowledge for Himself as well as for human being. He(سبحانه وتعلى) says about Himself:

﴿...عَلِمَ اللَّهُ أَنَّكُمْ سَتَذْكُرُونَهُنَّ...﴾[31]

"Allah knows that you will remember them."

About the human being, He(سبحانه وتعلى) says:

﴿...فَإِنْ عَلِمْتُمُوهُنَّ مُؤْمِنَاتٍ فَلا تَرْجِعُوهُنَّ إِلَى الْكُفَّارِ لا هُنَّ حِلٌّ لَّهُمْ وَلا هُمْ يَحِلُّونَ لَهُنَّ...﴾[32]

"Then if you ascertain that they are true believers, send them not back to the disbelievers, they are not lawful (wives) for the disbelievers nor are the disbelievers lawful (husbands) for them."

However, the knowledge attributed to a human being is not like that attributed to Allah (سبحانه وتعالى), as Allah(سبحانه وتعلى) says about Himself:

﴿...وَسِعَ كُلَّ شَيْءٍ عِلْمًا﴾[33]

"He has full knowledge of all things."

He also says:

﴿إِنَّ اللَّهَ لاَ يَخْفَى عَلَيْهِ شَيْءٌ فِي الأَرْضِ وَلاَ فِي السَّمَاءِ﴾[34]

"Truly, nothing is hidden from Allah, in the earth or in the heavens."

He(سبحانه وتعلى) says about human knowledge:

﴿...وَمَا أُوتِيتُم مِّن الْعِلْمِ إِلاَّ قَلِيلاً﴾[35]

[31] Al-Baqarah: 235
[32] Al-Mumtahinah: 10
[33] Al-Taha: 98
[34] Al-Imran: 5

"And of knowledge, you (mankind) have been given only a little."

Logical Evidence

It is well known logically, that meanings and attributes are understood according to the context in which they are found, just as things are different in their essence; likewise, they are different with respect to their characteristics and connotations surrounding them. Therefore, the characteristic feature of anything is adequate for it and cannot give either inadequate or excess information about the thing. For this, when we characterize a person or melting iron as being soft, we know that softness is of different degrees depending on the object being described as soft.

Sensible Proof

Looking at the elephant, we can see it has a body, legs and strength. Likewise, the mosquito also has a body, legs, and strength. However, we know the difference between their bodies, legs, and strength.

Based on this, It is clear to us that sharing similar names and attributes in some creatures does not imply that they are similar in essence; although all of them are accessible creatures. Therefore, none-resemblance in that regard between the Creator and the creature is even more pertinent and evident; indeed, the resemblance between the Creator and the creature is greatly impossible.

---

[35] Al-Isra': 85

Those who deviate from the Path of the Prophets

Concerning the Names and Attributes of Allah, (سبحانه وتعالى) those who deviate from the Path of the Prophets and others who follow their approach are of two categories: al- Mumaththila and Mu'atilah.

Each of these groups exaggerates in one aspect and neglects in another. For example, the Mumaththila exaggerates in the affirmation aspect and neglected in the negation aspect. Similarly, the people of the Mu'atilah exaggerated in the negation aspect. But they neglected in the affirmation aspect. Consequently, both of them failed to maintain balance in the two aspects of affirmation and negation.

The first group: al-Mumaththila

Their approach is an affirmation of Attributes of Allah (سبحانه وتعالى) in a way they resemble the attributes of the creatures; so they say: Allah(سبحانه وتعالى) has a face like our face, He has two hands like our hands, and He has two eyes like our eyes, and so on.

The reason behind their confusion is that Allah (سبحانه وتعالى) addresses us in the Qur'an by what we are able to understand and perceive. They say: we only understand what could be observed by us; therefore, if He addresses us about some things in the unseen, then we have no option than to perceive it according to what we know from the visible world.

Their approach is invalid and refuted by the textual, rational and sensible evidence.

Textual Proof:

Allah(**سبحانه وتعلى**) says:

﴿لَيْسَ كَمِثْلِهِ شَيْءٌ وَهُوَ السَّمِيعُ الْبَصِيرُ﴾[36]

"There is nothing like unto Him, and He is the All-Hearer, the All-Seer."

In another verse, Allah(**سبحانه وتعلى**) says:

﴿فَلاَ تَضْرِبُواْ لِلّهِ الأَمْثَالَ﴾[37]

"So put not forward similitudes for Allah."

Here, the first verse negates any possible resemblance; at the same time, it affirms the attributes of hearing and seeing for Allah(**سبحانه وتعلى**). The second verse affirms the prohibition of resemblance, so it is a combination between negation and prohibition.

Rational Proof

Al-Tamtheel may be rationally refuted in many ways:

Firstly, the difference between the Creator and the creatures in essence and existence implies a difference in attributes; this is due to the fact that the attribute of every being is suitable for it as the meanings and attributes are distinguished according to what they are associated with.

Secondly, to draw a comparison between the Creator and the creatures implies imperfection of the Creator; because comparing the perfect with imperfect makes the perfectly imperfect.

---

[36] Ash-Shura: 11

[37] An-Nahl: 74

Thirdly, comparing the Creator with the creature implies the invalidity of true worship. This is because no sane person will humble himself or worship someone unless he is greater than the worshiper.

Sensible Evidence

Actually, we are witness to the fact that many creatures share the same names and attributes, yet they differ in essence; the elephant has body and strength, the mosquito also has body and strength but the difference between their bodies and strength is well known.

If such differences between the creatures are well taken, then its possibility between the Creator and the creature is even more pertinent and obvious. Indeed, differences between the Creator and the creatures must be admissible, and comparison between them must be met with the highest degree of rejection.

Their claim: " we are addressed in the Qur'an by what is reasonably understood."

Regarding their statement "Allah addresses us in the Qur'an by what can be reasonably understood." This statement is true for the following verses of the Quran:

As Allah(**سبحانه وتعلى**) says:

﴿إِنَّا جَعَلْنَاهُ قُرْآنًا عَرَبِيًّا لَّعَلَّكُمْ تَعْقِلُونَ﴾[38]

[38] Az-Zukhruf: 3

"We verily, have made it a Qur'an in Arabic, that you may be able to understand."

And He(**سبحانه وتعلى**) says:

﴿كِتَابٌ أَنزَلْنَاهُ إِلَيْكَ مُبَارَكٌ لِّيَدَّبَّرُوا آيَاتِهِ وَلِيَتَذَكَّرَ أُوْلُوا الأَلْبَابِ﴾[39]

"(This is) a Book (the Qur'an) which We have sent down to you, full of blessings that they may ponder over its Verses, and that men of understanding may remember."

Allah(سبحانه وتعلى) also says:

﴿وَمَا أَرْسَلْنَا مِن رَّسُولٍ إِلاَّ بِلِسَانِ قَوْمِهِ لِيُبَيِّنَ لَهُمْ﴾[40]

"And We sent not a Messenger except with the language of his people, in order that he might make (the Message) clear for them."

If Allah (سبحانه وتعالى)did not wish for His slaves to understand what His Messengers came with, then it would not have been necessary to send it in the native language of the prophets' people. In that case, [any language would have been sufficient], whether their native language or any other language, any of them would serve the same purpose. However, the message would not have been made clear to the people; thus, it cannot be used as a proof against his creation [for their disobedience].

[39] Sad: 29
[40] Ibraheem: 4

Their claim: Messages must be perceived as known in the visible world,"

As to their statement, "If He addresses us about some things in the unseen, then we have to perceive it according to what we know from the visible world," the response could be from two perspectives:

The information was given by Allah (سبحانه وتعالى)about Himself is associated with His Glorified self; therefore, it should be uniquely for Him devoid of any suitability for His creatures. It is impossible for anyone to understand from this information 'similitude,' except those who do not have proper knowledge about Allah (سبحانه وتعالى)those who did not value Him as He should be valued, and those who comprehended not, the real message from the text as entailed by the context.

It is impossible that similitude is intended by
Allah (سبحانه وتعالى); because similitude between the creator and the creatures necessitates imperfection of the creator, and to believe that the creator is imperfect amounts to Kufur (disbelief) and aberration. And surely it is impossible that, disbelieve and aberration are intended by Allah(سبحانه وتعالى)with his words, rather He wants to save His servants from these. Allah(سبحانه وتعلى) says:

﴿يُبَيِّنُ اللَّهُ لَكُمْ أَن تَضِلُّواْ﴾[41]

"(Thus) does Allah makes clear to you (His Law) lest you go astray."

---

[41] Al-Nisa: 176

In another place, He(سبحانه وتعلى) says:

﴿وَلا يَرْضَى لِعِبَادِهِ الْكُفْرَ﴾[42]

"He likes not disbelief for His slaves."

The Second Group:[43] **Al-Mu'attilah and its Categories:** These are the group of people who entirely or partially deny the names and attributes established by Allah (سبحانه وتعالى) for Himself. To achieve this, they distort the texts of the Qur'an and Sunnah. Indeed, they are falsifiers of the texts [of the Qur'an and Sunnah] and deniers of Allah (سبحانه وتعالى)'s Attributes. These people are divided into four categories:

The First Category of Al-Mu'athilah: Al-'Asha'irah

Al-'Asha'irah those that share a similar belief with them, - Al-Mâtureediyyah and others- affirm the Names of

Allah (سبحانه وتعالى)and some of His Attributes; however, they deny the essence of many of these Attributes. Thus, they reject textual evidence which they think can be rejected, and distort -in the name of 'Al-Ta'wil (interpretation) - all Attributes of Allah (سبحانه وتعالى).

Attributes affirmed by Al-Asha'irah They affirmed seven Attributes: Life, Knowledge, Power, Will, Speech, Hearing and Seeing. Although

[42] Az-Zumar: 7

[43] The second group of Misguided people from the right path.

they differ with the Salaf in approach, concerning affirmation of some of these attributes.

Their confusion concerning this approach

They believe that affirmation of the denied attributes implies al-Tashbeeh meaning al-Tamtheel [which is a comparison between Allah and His creatures].

They argued concerning the affirmed [seven] attributes: Life, Knowledge, Power, Will, and Speech, Hearing and Seeing that the affirmation is logically supported as they claimed that:

1) Bringing about the created beings indicates the attribute of Power.
2) Characterization of some of the created being different from others indicates the attribute of Will.
3) Perfection in the process of creation indicates Knowledge.
4) These Attributes – Power, Will and Knowledge – imply Life, because these Attributes cannot exist except in a living being.
5) Any living being is either capable of speech, hearing and seeing characteristics which are attributes of perfection or impaired of these characteristics (muteness, deafness and blindness) which are attributes of imperfection. The latter attributes are not permissible for Allah(سبحانه وتعالى)as a result; the characteristics of speech, hearing and seeing must be affirmed.

Refutation of this approach

This approach may be refuted as follows:

1) Resorting to the intellect in this matter is a clear deviation from the approach of Salaf of this Ummah -the companions, the followers and the righteous Imams after them. None of them ever resorted to the intellect in this matter; on the contrary, they used to refer to the Qur'an and Sunnah. Therefore, they affirm the names and attributes affirmed by Allah (سبحانه وتعالى) about Himself or affirmed about Him by His messengers, an affirmation without Tamtheel and glorification without Ta'teel.
   - Imam of Ahl al-Sunnah, Ahmad bin Hanbal said: 'We attribute to Allah(سبحانه وتعالى)at He attributes to Himself, without going beyond the teachings of the Qur'an and Sunnah.'
2) Resorting to the intellect in this matter is illogical. This is because these are metaphysical issues or issues of the unseen world where there is no role for the intellect to play; rather, these can only be understood through revealed knowledge, [the Qur'an and Sunnah.]; therefore it is intellectually impossible to comprehend in details what is imperative or permissible or prohibited to believe with respect to Allah. Allah (سبحانه وتعالى) Therefore, allowing the intellect to judge in this issue contradicts the same intellect.
3) To resort to intellect in this matter is an invitation to disagreements and contradictions; because every individual is

endowed with an independent intellect, he believed should be resorted to as the case with these people. One may affirm what another denies, and perhaps the same person may contradict himself, by affirmation of something he denied in another place or denied something similar to it in another place. Indeed, there is no consistent code adopted by them to justify their opinions.

- Ibn Taymiyah said in his "Al-Fatwa al-Hamawiyyah": “I wish I knew by which intellect both the Qur’an and Sunnah are measured, may Allah(سبحانه وتعالى) be pleased with Imam Malik bin Anas, who said: “why is it that whenever a man is more dialectical than another we disregard what Jibril has brought down to Mohammad because of the arguments of those people.” It is known that making contradicting statements is indicative of being baseless.

4) Whenever they distort the meaning of revealed texts from its literal meaning to the meaning claimed by them to be logical, they are inevitably faced concerning the adopted meaning with the same problem faced concerning the rejected meaning. In addition to that, they have committed the crime of distorting the texts of the Qur’an and Sunnah as demonstrated below:

- If they argue that: the hand of Allah(سبحانه وتعالى)denotes the power of Allah (سبحانه وتعالى)and not the real hand because affirmation of real hand for Allah implies comparing Him with the creature attributed with a hand.

- In response to that, we say: Affirmation of 'Power' attracts the same problem attracted by affirmation of real hand. This is because creatures also have power; therefore, according to your rule, affirmation of Power for Allah (سبحانه وتعالى)also attracts likening Him to His creatures.
- If they say: 'Mahabbah (love) as an attribute of Allah connotes Allah'(سبحانه وتعالى)s wish to reward the beloved or connotes the reward itself and not the real love; because affirmation of the real meaning of Mahabbah (love) implies a comparison.
- In response to them, we say: If you interpret the al-Mahabbah with 'wish,' you are compelled with the same thing you are compelled in affirmation of al-Mahabbah (real love; because creatures also have a wish, so according to your rule, affirmation of wish for Allah also attracts comparing Him with the creatures. Likewise, if you interpret the 'Mahabbah' with reward, the reward is created and brought into being, which cannot be found except in a creator who made it. In addition to that, the maker must have a wish and intention to make. Therefore, according to your own rule, affirmation of the wish also implies comparing Allah(سبحانه وتعالى)with His creatures.
- Furthermore, we say also: your affirmation of the 'wish to reward' or 'reward' itself implies the love for the rewarded action. If not for the love for this action, the actor would not

have been rewarded. Based on that, your interpretation is also implied in what you have denied. If you affirm this attribute as compared to the creatures, then you have involved in al-Tamtheel (comparing the creator with the creatures), if you affirm it in the manner that is pertinent and appropriate for Allah (سبحانه وتعالى)then that will be correct and you must then affirm all other Attributes of Allah (سبحانه وتعالى) in the same manner.

5) Their argument regarding the denied attributes that: their (the attributes) affirmation implies comparison is unacceptable; as previously established, that sharing the same names and attributes does not imply similitude between the bearers of the names and the attributes. More so, this argument is rendered invalid by their affirmation of some Attributes for

Allah (سبحانه وتعالى); because they have affirmed for Allah(سبحانه وتعالى)the attributes of Life, Knowledge, Power, Wish, Speech, Hearing and Seeing, although the creatures have all of these characteristics as well. Therefore, according to their rule, affirming these Attributes for Allah (سبحانه وتعالى)implies comparison [between Allah and His creatures]

- If they respond by saying: We are affirming these Attributes for Allah (سبحانه وتعالى) in a manner that is pertinent to Him and is not like the ones affirmed for the creatures .
- In response, we say: This is a good and perfect answer, so why don't you say the same thing about the Attributes that

you have denied about Allah (سبحانه وتعالى) by affirming them for Him in a way most suitable and perfect for Him, without resembling what is affirmed for the creatures?

- If they respond by saying: What we have affirmed is logically supported; therefore, it has to be affirmed .This can be addressed as follows:

Firstly, it is not correct to depend on the intellect to address this issue, as we explained earlier.

Secondly, that affirmation of what you have logically denied is quite possible, which will –in some cases- be even more evident than some of the evidences you relied upon to affirm what you have affirmed, as the mercy that Allah(سبحانه وتعالى) has affirmed for Himself,

by saying: ﴿وَرَبُّكَ الْغَفُورُ ذُو الرَّحْمَةِ﴾[44] "And your Lord is Most Forgiving, Owner of Mercy, " and also saying:

﴿وَهُوَ الْغَفُورُ الرَّحِيمُ﴾[45] And He is the all-Forgiving, Most Merciful."

It is possible to logically affirm the attribute of being merciful as affirmed by textual evidence. This can be explained by saying: kindness to the creatures by granting them what is of benefit to them and protecting them from harm is indicative of being merciful just like His characterization of creatures is indicative of His attribute of 'Will'. It is even more evident and clearer than the indication of the 'Will' for being well-known to everyone.

---

[44] Al-Kahf: 58
[45] Yoonus: 107

Thirdly, on assumption that what you have denied cannot be logically affirmed, the fact that it cannot be logically affirmed does not in the actual sense of it implies nonentity. This is because the absence of a specific evidence to establish something does not necessarily mean the absence of the thing itself, as it may be affirmed by evidence. For the sake of argument, let us agree that it cannot be logically affirmed, but it has been affirmed by textual evidence, then we should affirm it by the existing uncontradicted or opposed evidence.

- If they argue that: its nonentity has logically indicated, as its affirmation implies comparison which is logically rejected.
- We respond by saying: If the affirmation of this implies comparison, then what you have affirmed also implies a comparison. If you deny similitude of the Attributes you have affirmed, you should also deny it here, because there is no difference between them. Based on that, you are left with only two options: you either accept affirmation in general as the Salaf did, or you accept negation in general as Mu'tazila and their cohorts did. Doing anything short of that by discriminating between the two issues (accepting affirmation for some and negation for others), is a clear contradiction.

The Second Category of Al-Mu'athilah: Al-Mu'tazilah and their followers

Al-Mu'tazilah and those who follow them such as scholastic theologians and others

Their approach towards the Names of Allah(سبحانه وتعالى)

- Their approach is to affirm for Allah(سبحانه وتعالى)Names without entailed Attributes by claiming that the Names of Allah (سبحانه وتعالى)are proper names, even some of them are of the opinion that these are synonyms, so, such names as al-'Aleem (All-knower), al-Qadeer (All-powerful), al-Samee' (All-Hearer) and al-Baseer (All-Seer) are synonymous to one another. Some others believe they are not synonyms; however, they hold the view that He is Knower without knowledge, powerful without power, Hearer without hearing and Seer without seeing and so on.

Their confusion regarding this approach

- They are confused on the basis of their belief that affirmation of these Attributes implies comparison; because (according to them) there is nothing that bears attribute without being a body and bodies resemble one another; therefore, affirming the Attributes implies similitude. This can be refuted as follows:

1) Allah (سبحانه وتعالى)has affirmed for Himself various Names and Attributes, it follows that if affirmation of the attributes

implies comparison, the same should be said of affirmation of the names. If affirmation of the names does not imply comparison then affirmation of the Attributes shall not imply comparison and to draw a difference between this and that is contradictory. To avoid this contradiction they should affirm all as Salaf did or deny all as the extremists among al-Jahmiyyah and al-Batiniyyah did. However, to differentiate between them would be contradictory.

2) Allah (سبحانه وتعالى)describes His Names as Husna (beautiful) and He commands us to invoke these Names.

He says: [46]﴿وَلِلَّهِ الأَسْمَاء الْحُسْنَى فَادْعُوهُ بِهَا﴾

"And (all) the Most Beautiful Names belong to Allah, so call on Him by them".

This implies that the names are of great meanings which can be used as Wasilah (means) in our Du'a (supplication), so, it is not right to claim that the names are devoid of meanings. If they are purely proper names, they would not have been indicative of any meaning except identification of its bearer [of the names], not to mention being Husna or Wasilah [means] in supplication .That Allah(سبحانه وتعالى)has without comparison affirmed for Himself the various Attributes both in brief as well as in details. Allah(سبحانه وتعالى) says:

[47]﴿وَلِلَّهِ الْمَثَلُ الأَعْلَىَ﴾ "And for Allah is the highest description."

[46] Al-A'raf: 180

[47] An-Nahl: 60

And He(سبحانه وتعالى) says:

﴿لَيْسَ كَمِثْلِهِ شَيْءٌ وَهُوَ السَّمِيعُ الْبَصِيرُ﴾[48]

"There is nothing like unto Him, and He is the All-Hearer, the All-Seer."

3) This indicates that affirmation of the attributes does not imply a comparison. If this implies comparison then the words of Allah(سبحانه وتعالى)would be contradicting.

4) Whoever is not of the qualities of perfection does not deserve to be called Rabb or Ilah. That is why Ibrahim faulted his father for adopting a non-hearing and non-seeing being as an object of worship by saying

﴿يَا أَبَتِ لِمَ تَعْبُدُ مَا لا يَسْمَعُ وَلا يُبْصِرُ وَلا يُغْنِي عَنكَ شَيْئًا﴾[49]

"O my father! Why do you worship that which hears not, sees not and cannot avail you in anything?"

5) Every existing being must have characteristic, indeed, no being can exist without having characteristic; therefore,

Allah (سبحانه وتعالى)the Creator, and the Supreme being must be a bearer of appropriate and perfect characteristics.

6) The claim that Allah's names are only proper names and synonyms, so they are simply indicative of the essence of Allah (سبحانه وتعالى), is invalid; because there are many pieces of evidence in the Qur'an and Sunnah indicating that each of these names has its own peculiar meaning, though they all

[48] Ash-Shura: 11

[49] Maryam: 42

indicate a single bearer of each name and a single bearer of each attribute. So Allah (سبحانه وتعالى)is Al-Hayyu (The ever-living) Al-Qiyyeem (the Self-subsisting by Whom all subsist), Al-Samee'(All-Hearer), Al-Baseer (All-seer), Al-'Aleem (All-knower) and Al-Qadeer (All-powerful). The bearer of the names and attributes is one yet the names and the attributes are numerous. Don't you see that Allah (سبحانه وتعالى)may affirm for Himself two or more names in the same place?

As He (سبحانه وتعالى)says:

﴿هُوَ اللَّهُ الَّذِي لا إِلَهَ إِلاَّ هُوَ الْمَلِكُ الْقُدُّوسُ السَّلامُ الْمُؤْمِنُ الْمُهَيْمِنُ الْعَزِيزُ الْجَبَّارُ الْمُتَكَبِّرُ﴾[50]

"He is Allah than Whom there is La ilaha illa Huwa (none has the right to be worshipped but He) the King, the Holy, the One Free from all defects, the Giver of security, the Watcher over His creatures, the All-Mighty, the Compeller, the Supreme".

If all of these names are only proper names, purely synonyms of one another, then stating all of these names in the same place is nonsensical, for being devoid of benefit.

7) The statement that Allah is a Knower without knowledge, Powerful without power, Hearer without hearing and Seer without seeing and so on" is a baseless statement, not in conformity with the standard of any language, be it Arabic or any other languages. It is a known fact that in all languages of

[50] Al-Hashr: 23

the world any derived word bears the meaning of the root word from which is derived. Therefore, it is impossible to say that someone is knowledgeable yet has no knowledge, or powerful yet has no power or hearer yet has no sense of hearing and so on. If this is the case, then

Allah (سبحانه وتعالى)'s names should be indicative of their appropriate Attributes. Therefore, the Names and Attributes must be affirmed for the Creator of Heaven and Earth.

8) Their argument that no bearer of attributes exists without being a body, is unacceptable; because there are many things which are not physically in existence, yet they have attributes, such as 'long night', 'short day', 'severe cold' and 'mild heat' …etc.; yet, these things are not bodies. In addition to that, associating the word al-Jism [body] with Allah whether in affirmation or denial is one of the heretical approaches adopted by the Ahl-al-Ta'teel to deny the Attributes affirmed by Allah(سبحانه وتعالى)about Himself.

9) Their argument that the bodies are uniform' is clearly invalid as disparity among bodies is evidently undeniable. The Shaykh, [the author] said: "there is no doubt that their claim about the uniformity of the bodies is an invalid argument."

The Third Category of Al-Mu'athilah

The Extremist among Jahmiyyah, Al-Qarâmitah, Al-Batiniyyah and their followers

Their approach towards the Names and the Attributes of Allah

- Their approach is that, they deny the Names as well as the Attributes and they do not attribute to Allah(سبحانه وتعالى) any attribute except by negation and not by affirmation. According to them:
    1) Allah (سبحانه وتعالى) is an absolute being, who cannot be characterized with any affirmative attribute, [because attributes restrict its bearer]. Therefore, it is not allowed to say: Allah exists, He is living, He is knowledgeable or He is powerful; as these are only attributes of His creatures.
    2) That they [these attributes] are metaphorical. Therefore affirmation of these attributes implies comparison with a knowledgeable and powerful living being, They also claim that the attribute is actually the same as its bearer, every attribute is the same as the other attribute; there is no difference between knowledge and power, or between hearing and seeing etc.

Their confusion

Their confusion concerning this issue is based on the belief that affirmation of the Names and Attributes implies comparison and plurality. To demonstrate this:

1) Concerning the names they claim: if a name is affirmed for Him, the meaning of that name must be attributed to Him.

For example, if we affirm for Him the name "Al-Hayy" [The Living], then it will imply that the attribute of life must be attributed to Him; because the authenticity of the derived noun implies the authenticity of the root verb from which it is derived. This implies that the attributes are attributed to it, so that is a comparison.

2) In the Attributes: they argue that affirmation of heterogeneous attributes which are different from the bearer of the attributes implies plurality. It is a type of an impossible combination, which is not in tandem with Tawheed.

Refutation of this approach

1) That Allah (سبحانه وتعالى)has combined both affirmation and negation in Names and Attributes He attributed to Himself. This has been previously explained with an example. Therefore, whoever acknowledges negation and denies affirmation, falls into the category of those who believe in part of the book and rejects the rest. Partial disbelieve in the book amounts to outright disbelieve in the book.

- Allah (سبحانه وتعالى)says in repudiating the children of Israel:

﴿أَفَتُؤْمِنُونَ بِبَعْضِ الْكِتَابِ وَتَكْفُرُونَ بِبَعْضٍ فَمَا جَزَاء مَن يَفْعَلُ ذَلِكَ مِنكُمْ إِلاَّ خِزْيٌ فِي الْحَيَاةِ الدُّنْيَا وَيَوْمَ الْقِيَامَةِ يُرَدُّونَ إِلَى أَشَدِّ الْعَذَابِ وَمَا اللَّهُ بِغَافِلٍ عَمَّا تَعْمَلُونَ﴾[51]

"Then do you believe in a part of the Scripture and reject the rest? Then what is the recompense of those who do so among

[51] Al-Baqarah: 85

you, except disgrace in the life of this world, and on the Day of Resurrection they shall be consigned to the most grievous torment. And Allah is not unaware of what you do."

- Allah(سبحانه وتعالى)also says:

﴿إِنَّ الَّذِينَ يَكْفُرُونَ بِاللَّهِ وَرُسُلِهِ وَيُرِيدُونَ أَن يُفَرِّقُواْ بَيْنَ اللَّهِ وَرُسُلِهِ وَيَقُولُونَ نُؤْمِنُ بِبَعْضٍ وَنَكْفُرُ بِبَعْضٍ وَيُرِيدُونَ أَن يَتَّخِذُواْ بَيْنَ ذَلِكَ سَبِيلاً * أُوْلَئِكَ هُمُ الْكَافِرُونَ حَقًّا وَأَعْتَدْنَا لِلْكَافِرِينَ عَذَابًا مُّهِينًا﴾[52]

"Verily, those who disbelieve in Allah and His Messengers and wish to make a distinction between Allah and His Messengers (by believing in Allah and disbelieving in His Messengers) saying: "We believe in some but reject others," and wish to adopt a way in between. They are in truth disbelievers. And We have prepared for the disbelievers a humiliating torment".

2) The absolute being without any attribute does not have existedin this physical world. It is only an assumption made by the mind, which has no existence in reality. Therefore, this argument essentially amounts to the denial of the existence of Allah (سبحانه وتعالى)except in the mind, which is actually the highest form of Al-Ta'teel and disbelief.

3) Their argument that the attribute is none other than its bearer and that every attribute is identical with another attribute, is logically unreasonable contention and flawed method of argumentation concerning a fundamental truth. It is known by virtue of the intellect and the senses that the attribute is not

[52] Nisa: 150-151

selfsame of its bearer, and that each attributes not identical to other. Knowledge is not the knowledgeable person, power is not the powerful person and speech is not the speaker. Likewise, knowledge, power and speech are different from one another.

4) Attributing to Allah (سبحانه وتعالى)affirmative Attributes is more indicative of His perfection than attributing to Him negating Attributes. This is due to the fact that affirmation is existential in nature in which arrays of perfection are entailed. However, negation is none-existential in nature and does not entail perfection without being combined with affirmation. But this group of people does not accept a negation combined with affirmation.

5) Their argument that 'affirmation of heterogeneous attributes which are different from the bearer of the attributes implies plurality' is a baseless argument in sharp contrast to logic and the sense. Having many attributes does not imply a plurality of the bearer of the attributes. A person can be described as a living being, hearer, seer, intellectual and speaker…etc; yet, these characteristics do not imply his plurality.

6) Their argument about names that affirmation of the Names implies that He the meaning of the name must be attributed to Him, this, according to them implies a comparison.

- In response to this, we say: The implied meanings attributed to the affirmation of the names are appropriate attributes for Allah, not that which is impossible for Him. Sharing similar names and attributes does not imply the resemblance of the bearers of the names and the attributes.

7) Their argument concerning names that 'its affirmation implies comparing Him with other existing beings.'

   - The response is to say that the denial that is acceptable to them implies a comparison with nonexistent beings as implied by their argument, which is more offensive than comparing Him with existing beings. Then, they should either accept the affirmation, and thereby follow the Salaf, or reject the negation as they have rejected the affirmation, and thereby follow the extremist among Al-Qarâmitah, Al-Batiniyyah and others. However, differentiating between this and that is a clear contradiction.

The fourth Category of Al-Mu'athilah

This category includes more extreme philosophers, Al-Jahmiyyah, Al-Qarâmitah, Al-Batiniyyah and others.

Their approach towards the attributes of Allah

- This group denies both affirmation and negation about the attributes of Allah(سبحانه وتعالى)they deny His existence, and non-existence, life and death, knowledge and ignorance and other such things. They say, He is neither existing nor not existing, neither alive nor dead, and neither knowledgeable nor ignorant and so on.

- Their confusion is not unconnected their belief that affirmation of His Attributes implies comparing Him with existing beings; and denial of Attributes implies comparing Him non-existing beings.

Refutation of this approach

This can be refuted as follows:

1) Calling Allah(سبحانه وتعالى)or describing Him as He called and described Himself is no similitude and does not imply a comparison. Because sharing the same name and characteristic does not necessitate the named and described things to be similar. Simply calling it resemblance is nothing except than stirring confusion among general people. If we accept this false claim, then any claimant can simply name the right things with improper names, in order to divert the people from accepting the right thing.
2) Obviously, for al-Mawjood al-Mumkin (The contingent existent), there should be Wâjib al-wujood (The necessarily existent) who will bring it to existence. We know and witness the emergence of things; this emergence cannot take place without an originator and it cannot cause its own emergence by itself.

   Allah (سبحانه وتعالى) says:

﴿أَمْ خُلِقُوا مِنْ غَيْرِ شَيْءٍ أَمْ هُمُ الْخَالِقُونَ﴾[53]

"Were they created by nothing, or were they themselves the creators?"

It becomes imperative to understand from this verse that, it must have a creator who is necessarily existent and He is Allah (سبحانه وتعالى). Actually, there are two types of beings in existence (Al-Wujood)

- First: Azalee, Wâjib al-wujood Eternal; necessarily and independently existent by Himself (Allah)(سبحانه وتعالى)
- Second: Created, Possibly Existent, brought into being by another.
- That both of them share the trait of being in existence does not imply similarity in all aspect of existence, as necessarily existent (Allah) has His own peculiarity and the existence of created being has its own peculiarity.
- The existence of the Creator is necessarily eternal and is not created, everlasting never-ending. The existence of the creature is possible, coming into being from nonentity, liable to perish or end. Those who deny affirmation of the existing conformity and dissension between these two types, it behooves them to either consider all beings as necessarily existent and self-existing beings or consider them all as

[53] At-Toor: 35

created, possibly existent and brought into existence by another. Both of these opinions are wrong.

3) Their denial of the affirmation and the negation at the same time amounts to a denial of two opposites at the same time, which is impossible. This is due to the fact that two opposites cannot be both existing or not existing at the same time; rather, one should be existing while the other is not. This -according to their rule- implies comparing Allah(سبحانه وتعالى)with impossibilities, because it is not possible to describe something as existent and non-existent or as non-living and non-dead at the same time. It can only be an imagination in the mind of some people, which has nothing to do with the reality.

Describing Allah(سبحانه وتعالى)in this way despite being in sharp contrast with logical spontaneities clear disbelief in the message brought by the Prophet (peace and the blessing of Allah be upon him).

- If they argue that denial of two opposites is only impossible in things the two opposites are applicable to, but it is not impossible in things the two opposites are not applicable to, just like an inanimate object which can neither be attributed with hearing nor deafness; as it is possible to say is neither mindful nor hearing impaired. This can be refuted as follows:
  1) This is invalid concerning their claim of denying both the existence and the non-existence because their relationship is like the reciprocal relationship of negative and positive; the absence of one mandates the presence of the other. If anyone says: 'not

present,' it means absent and 'not absent' means present. It is not possible to say 'not present and not absent' at the same time.

2) Their statement about inanimate objects whereby they cannot be characterized with life, death, blindness, sight, hearing, deafness, and the like where there is negative correspondence, this is a mere technical statement which does not change the facts. This is refuted with:

- The proof that inanimate objects have been turned alive, as Allah(سبحانه وتعالى) has turned Musa's stick to a snake that swallows what the magicians had fabricated.
- Allah(سبحانه وتعالى)has also described the inanimate objects as dead in His saying:

﴿وَالَّذِينَ يَدْعُونَ مِن دُونِ اللَّهِ لاَ يَخْلُقُونَ شَيْئًا وَهُمْ يُخْلَقُونَ*أَمْوَاتٌ غَيْرُ أَحْيَاء وَمَا يَشْعُرُونَ أَيَّانَ يُبْعَثُونَ﴾

"Those whom they (the polytheists) invoke besides Allah have not created anything, but are themselves created. (They are) dead, lifeless, and they know not when they will be raised up".

- He has also foretold that the Earth will declare its information which about all what happened over it of good or evil. This implies that it [Earth] hears whatever is said and sees whatever is done upon it.

3) Whoever is characterized by the characteristics of perfection is more perfect than the one who cannot be characterized by it. Therefore, whoever can be characterized with the characteristics of knowledge, power, hearing and sight is more perfect, even if they are actually devoid of them than the one who cannot even be characterized with these. Your argument that

"Allah (سبحانه وتعالى)is not characterized with these" implies that He less privileged than a human being, who can be characterized with these; because you have likened Him to inanimate objects that cannot be characterized with these characteristics.

4) If it is impossible to deny existence and inexistence then negating even the possibility of accepting [such a description] is more absurd. Based on that, their argument that 'The Lord (Allah) can neither be characterized by existence nor non-existence implies likening Him to the greatest impossibilities.'

The Dangers incurred by these four Categories

- Based on what has been discussed, it is clear that the aforementioned four categories of al-Mu'athilah have incurred some dangers:
  1) Deviation from the right part of Salaf of this Ummah.
  2) Distortion of revealed texts from what is intended.

3) Changing the meaning of the revealed texts to untended meanings.
4) Denial of the perfect Attributes of Allah (سبحانه وتعالى)which are entailed by the revealed texts.
5) Contradiction in the approach adopted by them in what they have affirmed or negated.

Our admonition to each and every one of these categories

- Concerning affirmation: affirm what you have denied but without comparison, as you have affirmed what you affirmed, but without comparison.
- Concerning negation: deny what you have affirmed in fear of falling into comparison as you have denied what denied in fear of falling into comparison. Otherwise, your approach is contradictory.
- The decisive, consistent, none-contradictory opinion is the one adopted by the Salaf and Imams of this Ummah. This is the affirmation of the Names and Attributes affirmed by Allah (سبحانه وتعالى) for Himself, an affirmation without comparison and glorification without denial of His Attributes. Also Included is to interpret the revealed texts according to their apparent meanings, in a way that is appropriate for Allah(سبحانه وتعالى)without any Tahreef[54], Ta'teel[55], Takyeef[56] or

[54] Tahreef: Distorting the actual meanings of His attributes
[55] Ta'teel: Suspending the actual meanings of His attributes

Tamtheel[57]. This will be clarified through two principles, two examples, and a conclusion.

The two principles regarding the Affirmation of the Attribute of Allah (سبحانه وتعالى)

First principle

- Those who affirmed some attributes for Allah (سبحانه وتعالى) but denying other, must be told that what is said concerning some attributes must be maintained with respect to others, meaning that whoever affirms some of the attributes affirmed by

Allah (سبحانه وتعالى)for Himself, must be compelled to affirm other attributes. And whoever denies any of the attributes must be compelled to deny what he has already affirmed, otherwise he is contradictory. Examples are as follows:

1) When a person affirms the real attribute of 'Will' and denies the attribute of 'Anger' interpreting it (anger) to mean "the will to revenge" or to mean "the revenge" itself. The response to him is as follows:

    - There is no difference between the real "Will" you have affirmed and the real anger you have denied, because If affirmation of the real "Anger" implies comparison [as you think], affirmation of the real "Will" also implies a comparison.

[56] Takyeef: Asserting the kayf (how) regarding His attributes without evidence
[57] Tamtheel: Asserting an anthropomorphic meaning to His attributes

- If affirmation of the real "Will" does not imply comparison, so affirmation of the real Anger will not also imply a comparison. This is because what is said concerning one of them should be maintained with respect to the other. Based on this, it is required of you either to affirm or deny all of these attributes

2) If he says: the "Will" I affirmed does not imply comparison; because what I affirmed is the "Will" that is appropriate for Allah (سبحانه وتعالى)which bears no resemblance to the "will" of the creature.The response to him is as follows:

   - Affirm for Allah(سبحانه وتعالى)the Anger which appropriates for Him and bears no resemblance to the anger as an attribute of the creature

3) If he claims that, Anger is ebullition of the blood of the heart preparatory to revenge, which is not appropriate for Allah (سبحانه وتعالى). The response to him is as follows:

   - That "Will" is also the intention to realize the benefit and to avoid harm which is also not appropriate for Allah (سبحانه وتعالى).

4) If he argues that, this definition of "Will" is for the creature, but the Will of Allah (سبحانه وتعالى)is appropriate for Him. The response to him is as follows:

   - That your definition of "anger" is also applicable to the creature, but "anger" as an attribute of Allah (سبحانه وتعالى)is appropriate for Him. In the same vein, the same thing is also applicable to all attributes he denied, it should be said to him the same thing he said about the attributes he affirmed.

5) If he argues that, he affirmed what he affirmed; because is being logically supported.
   - Our response to him is the same three answers previously stated in response to the argument of the first group [Al-'Asha'irah].

Second principle

- As for those who acknowledge the essence –self-existent Dhat of Allah, but compare His attributes with that of creatures or deny them, they should know that:
  - What is applicable to Dhat is also applicable to the attributes. This means that whoever affirms

  Allah (سبحانه وتعالى)'s existence without comparing Him to the existence of the creatures, he should also affirm the Attributes of Allah(سبحانه وتعالى)without comparing them to that of the creatures; because what is said concerning attributes is also applicable with respect to Dhat (His existence). Those who compare the attributes of Allah or deny them, Mu'tazilah and others must be confronted with this principle.
  - Those who compare should be asked: why is it that you compare the attributes of Allah while you compare not His essence or His existence with that of the creatures? Are you not aware that the

discussion with respect to the attributes is an extension of the discussion concerning His essence or existence?

- Those who deny the attributes (Ahl al-Ta'teel) Do you not say that the Dhat of Allah(سبحانه وتعالى)bears no resemblance to that of the creature? You should also say that the Attributes of Allah (سبحانه وتعالى)bear no resemblance to the characteristics of the creature.

Example of this

- If someone asks, Allah (سبحانه وتعالى)ascends over al-'Arsh; so how is His ascension? He should be told that what is said with respect to the attributes is also applicable concerning the Dhat; so please inform us how is His Dhat?
- If he replies: we do not know how He is? Our response is that we also do not know how His ascension is. Then, he has no option except to acknowledge the real meaning of Istiwâ (ascension), which bears no resemblance to the Istiwâ of the creature, and without any knowledge of the nature of this Istiwâ (ascension), as they have acknowledged the essence or existence of Allah (سبحانه وتعالى)without bearing resemblance to that of the creature and without any knowledge of how it is; as Imam Malik, his teacher Rabi', and others stated concerning Istiwâ: al-Istiwâ is known, al-kayf (the description of how) is unknown, to believe in it is obligatory, and inquiring about it (mode of al-Istiwâ) is unprecedented.

The statement:"الاستواء معلوم" [al- Istiwâ is known]

- It means that it is known in the Arabic language, the language in which the Qur'an has been revealed. It has several meanings contingent upon the proposition predicated with.
  - When it is predicated with the proposition"على"it refers to 'stability' and 'height,' as

  Allah(سبحانه وتعالى)says:

  ﴿فَإِذَا اسْتَوَيْتَ أَنتَ وَمَن مَّعَكَ عَلَى الْفُلْكِ﴾ [58]

  "And when you have embarked on the ship, you and whoever is with you.

  He also says:

  ﴿لِتَسْتَوُوا عَلَى ظُهُورِهِ ثُمَّ تَذْكُرُوا نِعْمَةَ رَبِّكُمْ إِذَا اسْتَوَيْتُمْ﴾[59]

  "In order that you may mount firmly on their backs, and then may remember the Favor of your Lord when you mount thereon".

  - Therefore, Istiwâ of Allah(سبحانه وتعالى)on the 'Arsh [Throne] is His attribute of being above it in a way that is appropriate for Him; in a manner that is unknown to us. This is not denoting [His] absolute supremacy above the rest of the creation.

[58] Al-Mu'minun: 28.
[59] Az-Zukhruf: 13.

The statement"والكيف مجهول" [The mode is unknown]

- It means that the mode of His al-Istiwâ (ascension) on His al-'Arsh is unknown to us for three reasons:
    1) Allah (سبحانه وتعالى)informs us that He ascends over His 'Arsh, without informing us exactly how the ascension is.
    2) The knowledge regarding the mode of an attribute is an extension of the knowledge about the bearer of the attribute. Therefore, if we do not know mode concerning the essence or existence of Allah (سبحانه وتعالى)then it is impossible to know with respect to His Attributes.
    3) The true nature of anything (i.e. how it is) can never be exactly known except by seeing it or seeing something similar to it or through authentic information about it. However, none of these means of obtaining information is possible regarding the ascension of Allah(سبحانه وتعالى) on His 'Arsh.This indicates that our Salaf (classical scholars) affirmed for the ascension a mode which is not known to us.

The statement:"والإيمان به واجب"(Believing in it is obligatory)

- It means believing in it in this way is obligatory. Allah(سبحانه وتعالى)has attributed it to Himself, and he knows better about Himself, His speech is the most truthful and His report is the best of the report. His message contains perfect knowledge, absolute truth, the supremacy of will and excellence of eloquence and speech; therefore it becomes incumbent on us to accept it and believe in it.

The statement "والسؤال عنه بدعة" [Inquiring about it is Bid'ah]

- It means asking about 'how it is' is bid'ah; because this question was not known at the time of the Prophet neither was it known during the era of his righteous caliphs, even though it is a religious issue. Therefore, initiating such a question is bid'ah. Inquiring about issues of this nature is part of the features of the perpetrators of bid'ah.
- Additionally, this type of inquiry is not even possible to answer; therefore, this would be considered an extravagance in the religion. The Prophet said: "Ruined are those who insist on hardship in matters of the Faith."
- This statement about al- Istiwâ credited to Malik and his teacher should be replicated to explain other Attributes of Allah (سبحانه وتعالى)like His descending to the first haven as well as other attributes by saying: these attributes are known in terms of meaning, unknown in terms of the mode. To believe in them is obligatory and inquiring about the mode is bid'ah .

The Two Examples

The first is about the Bliss of al-Jannah while the second is about the description of the Soul.

- The bliss of al-Jannah: Allah (سبحانه وتعالى)informs us that in al-Jannah there are foods, drinks, dresses, spouses, palaces, dates, pomegranates, fruits, meat, wine, milk, honey, water, ornaments of gold, pearls, silver and many others. All of these are in fact true; they are, in terms of nomenclature and meaning similar to the things in this world, however, they are different from the ones in the heaven in reality.
  - As for its correspondence with the things in the earth in meaning, Allah(سبحانه وتعالى) says about Qur'an:

﴿إِنَّا جَعَلْنَاهُ قُرْآنًا عَرَبِيًّا لَّعَلَّكُمْ تَعْقِلُونَ﴾[60]

"We verily, have made it a Qur'an in Arabic, that you may be able to understand." Were it not for its conformity with what is in the earth in meaning, we would not have been able to understand or realize it.

  - As for the difference between them in reality, Allah(سبحانه وتعالى) says:

﴿فَلا تَعْلَمُ نَفْسٌ مَّا أُخْفِيَ لَهُم مِّن قُرَّةِ أَعْيُنٍ جَزَاء بِمَا كَانُوا يَعْمَلُونَ﴾[61]

"No person knows what is kept hidden for them of joy as a reward for what they used to do".

And Allah(سبحانه وتعالى)says in Hadith al-Qudsi:

"أعددت لعبادي الصالحين ما لا عين رأت، ولا أذن سمعت ولا خطر على قلب بشر"[62]

---

[60] Az-Zukhruf: 3
[61] As-Sajdah: 17
[62] Al-Bukhari, Chapter: begging of the creation, lesson: Attributes of the heaven, no. 3244.

"I have prepared [Jannah] for my righteous slaves which have never been seen by any eye, nor heard about it by any ear and no human mind can ever imagine it."

Ibn 'Abbas - may Allah be pleased with him – said: Nothing from the heavenly things exists in this world except in their names[63].

- If these names refer to the actually named things in al-Jannah, and their correspondence to other names in this world does not imply their correspondence to them in reality, indeed, there is huge difference between them, which nobody knows except Allah (سبحانه وتعالى) Therefore, the difference between the Creator and the creature should be even greater and more evident than the difference among the creatures; because the difference existing among the creatures is simply a difference between one creature and another creature; because differences between creations is simply between a creature and another like creature. Therefore, if these differences [among the creatures] are clear, then differences between the Creator and the creature should be even more apparent and pertinent. With respect to this context- Belief in Allah (سبحانه وتعالى) and in the last day-People are divided into three groups:

The First Group

[63] Tafsir at-Tabari (1/135).

- Those are the Salaf, Imams and their followers; they believe in what Allah(سبحانه وتعالى) said about Himself and the Hereafter, as Allah(سبحانه وتعالى)has informed them about it. They believe in its actual existence and that it is real, with their belief that there is a difference between the things that exist in this world and those in the Hereafter. They also believe that the differences between the attributes of Allah(سبحانه وتعالى) and the attributes of His creatures are greater and more pertinent, as Allah (سبحانه وتعالى)says:

﴿لَيْسَ كَمِثْلِهِ شَيْءٌ وَهُوَ السَّمِيعُ الْبَصِيرُ﴾[64]

"There is nothing like unto Him, and He is the All-Hearer, the All-Seer."

The Second Group

- The people of the Kalam [theologists]; they believe what Allah(سبحانه وتعالى)has informed about Hereafter, the reward and the punishment; however, but they deny many Attributes affirmed by

Allah(سبحانه وتعالى)for Himself.

The Third Group

- They are Qaramitah, Batiniyyah and the Philosophers; they do not believe what Allah(سبحانه وتعالى) has informed about Himself or about the Hereafter. In fact, they deny the real essences of both.

[64] Ash-Shura: 11

- Their belief about what Allah (سبحانه وتعالى)has informed about Himself and the Hereafter is that it is only imagination with no reality.
- As for the command and the prohibition, many of them interpret the commands and the prohibitions to mean esoteric meanings in sharp contrast to what is known to all Muslims. Some examples of this esoteric meanings are:

1. Salat: Salat is interpreted to mean knowing the secret of their Shaykhs.
2. Fasting means hiding the secrets of their Shaykhs.
3. Hajj means visiting their Shaykhs and other interpretations which are undoubtedly known in Islam as clear fabrication, disbelief and apostasy.
4. They also say: the Shari'ah [Islamic rules and regulations] is obligatory for the general public not for the special elite. When a person achieves the stage of al-'Arifin and al-Muhaqqiqin [special stages], then they are exempt from any Shari'ah obligations, and the prohibitions become permissible for them.

- Some of the Sufi people may belong in this group.
- The Batiniyyah are considered apostates, and all Muslims agree that they are more disbelievers than the Jews and the Christians because of their great apostasy and opposition to all of the Divine Laws.

The Second Example: The soul

- The soul which is the means of life is the closest thing to a person and is his foundation. It has been stated in the revealed texts that it [the soul] is taken out from the body and made to ascend to the heaven and then returned to the body again. Nobody denies its real existence whereas nobody knows its essence and reality exactly, except what they know through revealed texts only. They are greatly confused about its nature because they do not see anything similar to it.
  1) A group of theologists considers the soul as a body or part of it or one of its characteristics.
  2) Another group of philosophers gave it a description suitable only for something which is impossible to be in existence; They say it exists neither inside the body nor outside of it, neither attached to it nor separated from it; neither mobile nor fixed; neither ascends nor descends, and it is neither essential nor nonessential. They also say that it is neither inside the world nor outside of it; neither separated from it nor existing within it. They describe it as they have described Allah(سبحانه وتعالى)the necessarily existent (Wâjib al-Wajuud.)
  - If it is said to them: it is rationally impossible to prove this statement about the soul. They will say: It is possible, with the evidence that Universals are possibly in existence whereas they cannot be pointed out to.

However, they forgot that Universals exist as Universals only in the imagination of the mind, and not reality. Indeed, the mind can make up things in its imagination that does not actually exist outside. For example, it can imagine the absence of two opposites or their existence at the same time, though it is impossible.

Confusion of Theologists (Mutakallimun) and philosophers

- Take note that Theologists (Mutakallimun) and philosophers are seriously confused about the soul because of two reasons:
  1) Lack of proper knowledge about its characteristics as stated in the revealed texts.
  2) They see nothing comparable to it; as the soul neither belongs to the type of the body nor to the type of the substances or anything generated from it. It definitely from a type completely different from these types. Therefore, the philosophers describe it in a manner that is opposing to visible objects. On the other hand, the Mutakallimun put it in the same category as the visible objects. As a result, the approach of the philosophers amounts to ta'teel [Stripping] and the approach of Mutakallimun amounts to al- tamtheel [comparison]; so both of these approaches are wrong.
     - It is narrated from the Prophet, that he said: "When the soul is taken out, the eyes follow it, and the angels put it in a burial cloth, and go up with it to the heaven." However, its reality and nature is beyond our comprehension;

  as Allah(سبحانه وتعالى) says:

﴿وَيَسْأَلُونَكَ عَنِ الرُّوحِ قُلِ الرُّوحُ مِنْ أَمْرِ رَبِّي وَمَا أُوتِيتُم مِّن الْعِلْمِ إِلاَّ قَلِيلاً﴾[65]

“And they ask you (O Muhammad) concerning the Ruh (the Spirit); Say: "The Ruh (the Spirit): it is one of the things, the knowledge of which is only with my Lord. And of knowledge, you (mankind) have been given only a little".

Comparison between the mode of the soul and the mode of Allah's Attributes

- If the soul is proven to be a fact, and its description by the Qur’an and the Sunnah is real, although it does not resemble any visible object; then, for the Creator to be characterized by appropriate attributes of perfection with a clear difference from the creatures is more pertinent.
- The failure of the intellectuals to precisely describe Allah (سبحانه وتعالى) or to explain the mode of His Attributes is more glaring than their failure to describe the soul and explain its mode.
- If one who denies the characteristics of the soul is considered none believer in its existence and the one who compares it to the visible creatures is considered ignorant of the soul and guilty of al-Tamtheel, then he who denies the Attributes of Allah (سبحانه وتعالى) or compare them to that of creatures is guiltier to be considered a disbeliever a stripper of the attributes,

[65] Al-Isra’: 85

and he who compares Him to His creatures in ignorance is guiltier to be regarded as a comparer.

Conclusion

This conclusion contains many beneficial fundamental principles.

The First Principle

Allah (سبحانه وتعالى)is attributed by affirmation of affirmative attributes and by the negation of negative attributes.

- The meaning of this principle may be summarized as follows:

1) Allah(سبحانه وتعالى)combined both affirmation and negation in His description of Himself.

Allah(سبحانه وتعالى)says:

﴿لَيْسَ كَمِثْلِهِ شَيْءٌ وَهُوَ السَّمِيعُ الْبَصِيرُ﴾[66]

"There is nothing like unto Him, and He is the All-Hearer, the All-Seer."

2) Allah (سبحانه وتعالى)combined both affirmation and negation because the perfection of the bearer of the attributes can only be attained by negating derogatory attributes and affirmation of the attributes of perfection.

[66] Ash-Shura: 11

The attributes negated by Allah (سبحانه وتعالى)about Himself are all attributes of imperfection like fatigue, weariness, laziness, oppression and resemblance with the creature. In the same vein, all attributes affirmed by Allah(سبحانه وتعالى)about Himself are Attributes of perfection, He says :"And for Allah(سبحانه وتعالى)is the highest description." Whether these attributes are typical inherent attributes [الصفات الذاتية]which are His eternal and everlasting attributes or typical attributes of action[الصفات الفعلية] which are conditionally attributed to Him, though these attributes of action are originally affirmed for Him eternally and everlastingly, Allah (سبحانه وتعالى)has never and will never cease to be active.

The Attributes affirmed by Allah(سبحانه وتعالى) for Himself

Some of the Attributes affirmed by Allah(سبحانه وتعالى) for Himself are Life, Knowledge, Power, Hearing, Seeing, Will, Speech, Honor, Wisdom, Forgiveness and Mercy.

- **Life**: The Life as an attribute of Allah (سبحانه وتعالى)is a perfect life that entails all qualities of perfection, was neither preceded by nonentity nor will be followed by extinction. Allah(سبحانه وتعالى)says:

﴿وَتَوَكَّلْ عَلَى الْحَيِّ الَّذِي لا يَمُوتُ﴾[67]

"And put your trust (O Muhammad) in the Ever Living One Who dies not". Allah(سبحانه وتعالى) says:

﴿هُوَ الأَوَّلُ وَالآخِرُ﴾[68]

"He is the First (nothing is before Him) and the Last(nothing is after Him"). And
He (سبحانه وتعالى)says:

﴿اللَّهُ لاَ إِلَهَ إِلاَّ هُوَ الْحَيُّ الْقَيُّومُ لاَ تَأْخُذُهُ سِنَةٌ وَلاَ نَوْمٌ﴾[69]

"Allah! None has the right to be worshipped but He, the Ever-Living, the One Who sustains and protects all that exists. Neither slumber, nor sleep overtakes Him" .

- **Knowledge:** His Knowledge is perfect, inclusive of the knowledge of everything; big or small, close or far. His knowledge is neither preceded by ignorance nor will be followed by oblivion. As Allah(سبحانه وتعالى) narrates about Musa when he was asked by Fir'awn: what about the earlier generation?

﴿قَالَ عِلْمُهَا عِندَ رَبِّي فِي كِتَابٍ لَّا يَضِلُّ رَبِّي وَلا يَنسَى﴾[70]

"Musa (Moses)] said: 'The knowledge thereof is with my Lord, in a Record. My Lord is neither unaware nor He forgets." And He says:

---

[67] Al-Furqan: 58
[68] Al-Hadeed: 3
[69] Al-Baqarah: 255
[70] Taha: 52

﴿إِنَّ اللَّهَ بِكُلِّ شَيْءٍ عَلِيمٌ﴾[71]

"Verily, Allah is the All-Knower of everything."

- **Power**: His power is perfect is neither preceded with inability nor will be followed by fatigue. Allah (سبحانه وتعالى)says:

﴿وَمَا كَانَ اللَّهُ لِيُعْجِزَهُ مِن شَيْءٍ فِي السَّمَاوَاتِ وَلا فِي الأَرْضِ إِنَّهُ كَانَ عَلِيمًا قَدِيرًا﴾[72]

"Allah is not such that anything in the heavens or in the earth escapes Him. Verily, He is All-Knowing, All-Omnipotent".

He (سبحانه وتعالى)also says:

﴿لِتَعْلَمُوا أَنَّ اللَّهَ عَلَى كُلِّ شَيْءٍ قَدِيرٌ وَأَنَّ اللَّهَ قَدْ أَحَاطَ بِكُلِّ شَيْءٍ عِلْمًا﴾[73]

"That you may know that Allah has power over all things, and that Allah surrounds (comprehends) all things in (His) Knowledge.

He(سبحانه وتعالى) also says:

﴿وَلَقَدْ خَلَقْنَا السَّمَاوَاتِ وَالأَرْضَ وَمَا بَيْنَهُمَا فِي سِتَّةِ أَيَّامٍ وَمَا مَسَّنَا مِن لُّغُوبٍ﴾[74]

"And indeed We created the heavens and the earth and all between them in six Days and nothing of fatigue touched Us" .

- **Al-Hikmah** (wisdom): His wisdom is perfect and comprehensive; it is free from all forms of absurdity, and inclusive of His creation and legislation.

Allah(سبحانه وتعالى)says:

---

[71] Al-Anfal: 75
[72] Fatir: 44
[73] At-Talaq: 12
[74] Qaf: 38

﴿وَمَا خَلَقْنَا السَّمَاوَاتِ وَالأَرْضَ وَمَا بَيْنَهُمَا لاعِبِينَ * مَا خَلَقْنَاهُمَا إِلاَّ بِالْحَقِّ...﴾[75]

"And We created not the heavens and the earth, and all that is between them, for mere play * We created them not except with truth (i.e. to examine and test those who are obedient and those who are disobedient and then reward the obedient ones and punish the disobedient ones."

He(سبحانه وتعالى) also says:

﴿الَّذِي خَلَقَ الْمَوْتَ وَالْحَيَاةَ لِيَبْلُوَكُمْ أَيُّكُمْ أَحْسَنُ عَمَلاً﴾[76]

"Who has created death and life, that He may test you which of you is best indeed" .

He(سبحانه وتعالى) says:

﴿...ذَلِكُمْ حُكْمُ اللهِ يَحْكُمُ بَيْنَكُمْ وَاللَّهُ عَلِيمٌ حَكِيمٌ﴾[77]

His wisdom, like His other Attributes; the creatures are not fully aware of it. We may not be able to realize all the significance rationale behind what He has created or legislated, though we may know some, which Allah(سبحانه وتعالى) has disclosed to us.

- Likewise, all of His Attributes which He has affirmed for Himself are perfect, there is no deficiency therein in whatever form.

[75] Ad-Dukhan: 38-39
[76] Al-Mulk: 2
[77] Al-Mumtahinah: 10

The Attributes Negated by Allah (سبحانه وتعالى) for Himself

- The Attributes that Allah (سبحانه وتعالى)has negated for Himself are: death, ignorance, forgetfulness, inability, slumber, sleep, weariness, fatigue, and oppression.

1) **Death:**Allah(سبحانه وتعالى)says:

﴿وَتَوَكَّلْ عَلَى الْحَيِّ الَّذِي لا يَمُوتُ﴾[78]

"And put your trust (O Muhammad) in the Ever Living One Who dies not" .

2) **Forgetfulness:** He(سبحانه وتعالى) have stated about Musa:

﴿...فِي كِتَابٍ لّا يَضِلُّ رَبِّي وَلا يَنسَى﴾[79]

"In a Record, My Lord is neither unaware nor He forgets."

3) **Inability:** Allah(سبحانه وتعالى)says:

﴿وَمَا كَانَ اللَّهُ لِيُعْجِزَهُ مِن شَيْءٍ فِي السَّمَاوَاتِ وَلا فِي الأَرْضِ...﴾[80]

"Allah is not such that anything in the heavens or in the earth escapes Him".

4) **Sleep:** And He(سبحانه وتعالى)says:

﴿...لاَ تَأْخُذُهُ سِنَةٌ وَلاَ نَوْمٌ﴾[81]

"Neither slumber nor sleep overtakes Him" ".

5) **Fatigue:** He(سبحانه وتعالى) says:

---

[78] Al-Furqan: 58
[79] Taha: 52
[80] Fatir: 44
[81] Al-Baqarah: 255

﴿...وَمَا مَسَّنَا مِن لُّغُوبٍ﴾[82]

"And nothing of fatigue touched Us" .

6) **Weariness:** He(سبحانه وتعالى)says:

﴿...وَلَمْ يَعْيَ بِخَلْقِهِنَّ...﴾[83]

"And was not wearied by their creation" .

7) **Oppression:** He (سبحانه وتعالى)says:

﴿...وَلا يَظْلِمُ رَبُّكَ أَحَدًا﴾[84]

"And your Lord treats no one with injustice."

Issues involved in the attributes negated by Allah (سبحانه وتعالى) about Himself

- There are two issues involved in all of the attributes negated by Allah (سبحانه وتعالى)about Himself: Inappropriateness of the attributes and Veracity of its perfect opposites. both can be buttressed in the verse:

﴿وَمَا كَانَ اللَّهُ لِيُعْجِزَهُ مِن شَيْءٍ فِي السَّمَاوَاتِ وَلا فِي الأَرْضِ إِنَّهُ كَانَ عَلِيمًا قَدِيرًا﴾[85]

"Allah is not such that anything in the heavens or in the earth escapes Him. Verily, He is All-Knowing, All-Omnipotent. "

So, When Allah (سبحانه وتعالى)negates inability for Himself then he explains that it is because of His perfect Knowledge and Power . Based on this, it is clear to us that:

[82] Qaf: 38
[83] Al-Ahqaf: 33
[84] Al-Kahf: 49
[85] Fatir: 44

1) Negation of oppression signifies the attribute of His perfect Justice.
2) Negation of fatigue and weariness signifies the attribute of His perfect Power.
3) Negation of slumber and sleep signifies the attribute of His Absolute Life and supreme power of sustaining and protecting.
4) Negation of death signifies the attribute of His Everlasting Life; likewise, the same approach is applicable to all others negated attributes.

The nature of negation with respect to Allah's attributes

- The negation in attributes of Allah is not an absolute negation; in fact, it must be purposely to affirm His perfection, this is based on the following reasons:

1) Allah (سبحانه وتعالى)says:

﴿...وَلِلَّهِ الْمَثَلُ الأَعْلَىَ...﴾

"And for Allah is the highest description. "

This means perfection of His Attributes, and it cannot be found through absolute negation.

Absolute negation is essentially the absolute nonexistence of something and absolute nonexistence means nothing. And so, how can nothingness be praiseworthy and perfect?

2) Negation - if does not entail perfection – could be because this attribute or its opposite are not befitting with the One described; not necessarily due to the perfection of the One described. For example, if someone says: "The wall does not oppress," here, negating oppression of the wall does not refer to its perfection; rather, the attribute of injustice or justice is not suitable to describe the wall with it. Therefore, negating the attribute of oppression will neither be considered praiseworthy nor due to its perfection.
3) Negation of attribute, if it does not entail perfection, it could be due to the lack in quality of the bearer or his inability. For example, if the person who lacks the ability to protect himself from oppression is described: "he does not pay back evil with evil," so negation of vengeance, in this case, is not due to the bearer's perfect attribute of forgiveness; but due to his inability to protect himself. Based on that, acquitting him of this attribute indicates a lack in quality and humiliation, not perfection and commendation. Take the example of Hamasi satire of his tribe:
   - If I were from [the tribe of] Majin,, my camel would not have been seized by the children of al- Laqitah of Dhahl bin Shaiban

Until he said

- But my people, although they are many in number, in whatever form, they perpetrate not in evil even if they are disgraced.
- They reward the oppression of the oppressors with forgiveness and the evil of the evil doers with kindness.

The poet intended to satirize them and characterize them with inability not to praise them for their forgiveness; as indicated by his [following] line:

- I wish if I had [in their stead] a tribe when they are attacked, they invade [the enemy] by marching and riding horse.

With the above discussion, it should be known that those who only attribute to Allah (سبحانه وتعالى)absolute negation, are actually not affirming any Praiseworthy and worship deserving being, even a non-existing one; as they say about Allah(سبحانه وتعالى).

"He is neither inside the world nor outside of it, neither detached from it nor immanent within[86], neither above it nor below it, neither connected nor separated from it and so forth".

- That is the more reason why Mahmoud bin Sabakatakin[87] challenged those who[88] describe Allah (سبحانه وتعالى) in this manner by saying:

[86] See Ibn Qasim, Majmu' al-Fatwa (5/269).

[87] The author of the book notes here: Mahmoud ibn Sabakatakin, one of the notable leaders, the Secretary of the State and the Caretaker of the Religion, took over the government in the year 389 Hijri. The Abbasid Caliph, Al-Qadir Billah, sent him the gown of the sultanate [as a gift]. He opened the cities of Khurasaan and his kingdom stretched from India to Niasboor. He, originally a Turk, was eloquent,

"explain to us the difference between this Rabb that you have described and a nonexistent."

- He spoke the truth, may Allah(سبحانه وتعالى)bestow mercy upon him. Indeed, a non-existent could not have been described well than their description of the Creator. Therefore, whoever says: 'He is neither detached from the world nor does He exist within it' share the same position with those who say: 'He is neither independent nor dependent, He is neither eternal nor created; and that His existence neither precedes the world nor coexisting with it'. For those who say that: 'He is neither alive, nor a hearer, nor a seer, nor a speaker', that implies that He is dead, deaf, blind and dumb (be He exalted, far above all this).

The Second Principle

- We must believe in what Allah(سبحانه وتعالى)has informed us in His book, or what His Messenger has informed us, whether we know its meaning or not, due to the following reasons:

---

prudent, reasonable, and a courageous fighter. He opened many cities in India, which no other ruler was able to accomplish. Nonetheless, he was extremely religious and God-conscious, despising all disobediences, false amusements, and its people. He loved the scholars and the righteous, and would sit with them for discussions. He died in Ghuznah in the year 421-422 Hijri when he was sixty-three years old. He had then been a king for thirty-three years. May Allah have mercy on him.

[88] He is the famous theologian, Abu Bakr bin Fawrak.

1) Allah(سبحانه وتعالى)says:

﴿يَا أَيُّهَا الَّذِينَ آمَنُواْ آمِنُواْ بِاللّهِ وَرَسُولِهِ وَالْكِتَابِ الَّذِي نَزَّلَ عَلَى رَسُولِهِ وَالْكِتَابِ الَّذِيَ أَنزَلَ مِن قَبْلُ﴾[89]

"O you who believe! Believe in Allah, and His Messenger (Muhammad), and the Book (the Qur'an) which He has sent down to His Messenger, and the Scripture which He sent down to those before (him)" .

2) He(سبحانه وتعالى)also says:

﴿يَا أَيُّهَا النَّاسُ قَدْ جَاءَكُمُ الرَّسُولُ بِالْحَقِّ مِن رَّبِّكُمْ فَآمِنُواْ خَيْرًا لَّكُمْ وَإِن تَكْفُرُواْ فَإِنَّ لِلَّهِ مَا فِي السَّمَاوَاتِ وَالأَرْضِ وَكَانَ اللّهُ عَلِيمًا حَكِيمًا﴾[90]

" O mankind! Verily, there has come to you the Messenger (Muhammad) with the truth from your Lord, so believe in him, it is better for you. But if you disbelieve, then certainly to Allah belongs all that is in the heavens and the earth. And Allah is Ever All-Knowing, All-Wise" .

3) The message of Allah stems from absolute knowledge; indeed, He(سبحانه وتعالى) knows best about Himself as well as about others.

Allah(سبحانه وتعالى)says :

﴿...قُلْ أَأَنتُمْ أَعْلَمُ أَمِ اللّهُ...﴾[91]

" Say, Do you know better or does Allah."

[89] An-Nisa': 136
[90] An-Nisa': 170
[91] Al-Baqarah: 140

4) And because the message of Allah is the most truthful of news.

﴿...وَمَنْ أَصْدَقُ مِنَ اللَّهِ حَدِيثًا﴾[92]

" And who is truer in statement than Allah ".

The speech of Allah (سبحانه وتعالى)is the most lucid, most eloquent and clearest. As Allah(سبحانه وتعالى)says:

﴿وَلا يَأْتُونَكَ بِمَثَلٍ إِلاَّ جِئْنَاكَ بِالْحَقِّ وَأَحْسَنَ تَفْسِيرًا﴾[93]

"And no example or similitude do they bring (to oppose or to find fault in you or in this Qur'an), but We reveal to you the truth (against that similitude or example), and the better explanation thereof. "

And He(سبحانه وتعالى)says:

﴿اللَّهُ نَزَّلَ أَحْسَنَ الْحَدِيثِ كِتَابًا مُّتَشَابِهًا مَّثَانِيَ...﴾[94]

"Allah has sent down the best statement, a Book (this Qur'an), its parts resembling each other in goodness and truth, oft-repeated."

Resembling each other', meaning, they resemble each other in perfection and clarity.

Allah(سبحانه وتعالى)says:

﴿نَزَلَ بِهِ الرُّوحُ الأَمِينُ*عَلَى قَلْبِكَ لِتَكُونَ مِنَ الْمُنذِرِينَ *بِلِسَانٍ عَرَبِيٍّ مُّبِينٍ﴾[95]

---

[92] An-Nisa': 87
[93] Al-Furqan: 33
[94] Az-Zumar: 23

"Which the trustworthy Ruh [Jibrael (Gabriel)] has brought down * Upon your heart (O Muhammad) that you may be (one) of the warners * In the plain Arabic language."

5) Allah(سبحانه وتعالى)intends, with what He has sent down from revelation, for the people to be guided and not misguided. As Allah (سبحانه وتعالى)says:

﴿يُرِيدُ اللَّهُ لِيُبَيِّنَ لَكُمْ وَيَهْدِيَكُمْ سُنَنَ الَّذِينَ مِن قَبْلِكُمْ...﴾[96]

"Allah wishes to make clear (what is lawful and what is unlawful) to you, and to show you the ways of those before you."

And He(سبحانه وتعالى)says:

﴿...يُبَيِّنُ اللَّهُ لَكُمْ أَن تَضِلُّواْ وَاللَّهُ بِكُلِّ شَيْءٍ عَلِيمٌ﴾[97]

" (Thus) does Allah makes clear to you (His Law) lest you go astray. And Allah is the All-Knower of everything" .

- Likewise, we have to believe that the message related by the Prophet stems from knowledge; indeed, he is the most knowledgeable of people about His Lord, His Names, Attributes and legislation.
- His message is the most authentic of human messages; his speech of the most eloquent of human speeches; his intention is the best of human intentions; indeed, he is the most sincere admonisher for the Human and Jinn.

[95] As-Shu'ara': 193-195
[96] An-Nisa: 26
[97] An-Nisa: 176

- the message of Allah(سبحانه وتعالى)and the message of His messenger encompass absolute knowledge, truth, eloquence, perfect objective and will. These are the fundamental qualities for a message to be accepted message. That is why any information related by an ignorant person or a liar or unconscious or with bad intention, will not be accepted because for lacking fundamental qualities for acceptance or some of it.
- Thus, if all the fundamental qualities for a message to be accepted are satisfied and contained in a perfect form in the message given by Allah (سبحانه وتعالى)and His messenger, then it becomes incumbent to believe it and accept it, whether in the form of negation or affirmation. And so, there is no excuse for any apologist to reject it or to distort it or to doubt its content, especially about the Names and Attributes of Allah (سبحانه وتعالى). Likewise, what has been established by the consensus of the classical scholars [salaf] of this Ummah must be accepted. And most of the issues related to the subject of "the Names and the attributes of Allah (سبحانه وتعالى)are stipulated in the Qur'an and Sunnah and has been agreed upon by the early scholars of the Ummah.
- On the other hand, for those issues which are subject of controversy among the late generation of scholars, which are neither mentioned in the Qur'an and the Sunnah nor are they even mentioned by the Salaf of this Ummah, it is not mandatory even permissible for him to affirm or negate it; because it is not mentioned in the revealed texts.

Additionally, nobody should accept or reject its meaning until its true meaning becomes clear to him; if it is proven correct, it should be accepted; otherwise, it should be rejected. Some examples are as follow:

First Example: Al-jih'th(The Direction)

- If someone says: 'Allah is towards a direction or does Allah have direction? He should be answered by telling him: the word "direction" is not mentioned in the Qur'an or the Sunnah in the affirmative or the negative. There is no reference therein as to whether He is towards a direction, or that He has a direction, or whether He is towards a direction or He does not have direction. Instead, the revealed texts refer to what suffices Him of a description such as Highness, Above all else, ascension over al-'Arsh (or the Throne), and the ascension of things to Him and their descent from Him.

Opinions of late generation of scholars concerning affirmation of "Direction"

- The late generations of scholars were of diverse opinion with respect to affirmation or negation of this issue. If the just mentioned principle is applied we say:
  - As for the term, we will neither affirm it nor negate it; because it has never been mentioned before.

- Regarding its meaning, we should examine what is intended by the term "direction":

1. Is the term "direction" mean something created which surrounds Allah(سبحانه وتعالى) if so, then that is an invalid meaning, which is not appropriate for Allah (سبحانه وتعالى), as nothing of His creation can surround Him; in fact, His Kursi extends over the heavens and the earth, and He feels no fatigue in guarding and preserving them. Additionally, so, it is impossible for Him to be contained within any of His creatures.
2. If what is meant by "al-Jih'th" (direction), is that which is above the world, then it is right to be affirmed for Allah (سبحانه وتعالى)Indeed,

Allah (سبحانه وتعالى)is above His creation, higher than them, as it has been proven by the Qur'an, Sunnah, Ijma,' Intellect and Fitrah [innate nature]. In Sahih Muslim, it has been narrated by Mu'awiyah bin al-Hakam al-Salamy that

The Prophet ﷺ asked a slave owned by Mu'awiyah, "Where is Allah?" She replied: "In the Heaven." Then Prophet ﷺ asked, "Who am I?" She replied: "You are the Messenger of Allah". After that, Prophet ﷺ said: "Free her for she is a Mu'minah [believer]".[98]

---

[98] Narrated by Muslim, Book of Mosques and Prayer Places, Chapter: Talking in the Prayer is Unlawful, No. 537.

Second Example: Al-Hayyiz (Space) or Al-Mutahayyiz (Occupier of a space)

- If someone says: is it allowed to characterize Allah(سبحانه وتعالى)by saying: He is an occupier of a space (Mutahayyiz) or is in a space –encompassed by a space (Hayiz)?
- We respond by saying: both terms - Hayyiz and Tahayyuz - with respect to Allah, are neither affirmed nor denied in the Qur'an or the Sunnah. It is not found in both of them that He is in a space (Hayyiz) or is the occupier of a space (Mutahayyiz), or whether it is not so. Instead, it is found in the revealed texts what (attribute) is more sufficient than this, such as the Al-Kabir (the most Great) Almuta'l (the most High).

Opinions of late generation of scholars concerning affirmation of "Hayyiz" or "Mutahayyiz"

- The late generations of scholars were of diverse opinion with respect to affirmation or negation of this issue. If the just mentioned principle is applied we say:
  - As for the term, we will neither affirm it nor negate it; because it is not revealed in any of the divine text.
  - Regarding its meaning, we should examine what is intended by al-Hayyiz or at-Tahayyuz :
- Is the term "direction" mean something created which surrounds Allah(سبحانه وتعالى) if so, then that is an invalid meaning, which is

not appropriate for Allah (سبحانه وتعالى), as nothing of His creation can surround Him; in fact, His Kursi extends over the heavens and the earth, and He feels no fatigue in guarding and preserving them. Additionally, so, it is impossible for Him to be contained within any of His creatures.

1. If what is meant by "al-Hayyiz (space)", is that Allah is contained by His creatures and confined by them, then the meaning is invalid, and must be denied; as it is not appropriate for Allah. Indeed, Allah(سبحانه وتعالى) is so great, so mighty, more exalted than to be contained or confined by His creatures, more so that His Kursi extends over the Heavens and the Earth, and on the Day of Resurrection, the whole earth will be grasped by His Hand and the Heavens will be rolled up by His Right Hand? It has been reported in the book of al-Bukhari and Muslim (the Saheehayn), as well as in other sources, from the authentic narration of Abu Hurayrah in which he says: Prophet (peace and blessing of Allah be upon him) says: "On the Day of Resurrection, Allah(سبحانه وتعلى) will grasp the whole Earth and He will roll up the Heavens with His Right Hand. Then He shall say: I am The King; where are the kings of the Earth?"[99] Ibn 'Abbas says: "Indeed, the Seven Heavens and the Seven Earths and what is contained therein are nothing to Allah's

[99] Narrated in al-Bukhari, Book of Tafseer, Chapter وَالأَرْضُ جَمِيعًا قَبْضَتُهُ يَوْمَ الْقِيَامَةِ وَالسَّمَاوَاتُ مَطْوِيَّاتٌ بِيَمِينِهِ No. 4812. Narrated in Muslim, Book: The Description of The Day of Resurrection, No. 2787.

Hand but the like of a mustard seed in the hand of one of you".

2. If what is meant by Hayyiz or Mutahayyiz is that Allah(سبحانه وتعالى)is "Munheez" (distant) from His creation meaning; He is different from His creatures and separated from them, neither existing within them nor do they existing within Him. The meaning, in that case, is affirmed to be valid for Allah(سبحانه وتعالى). Indeed, the Imams of Ahl al-Sunnah say: He is above the seven Heavens on His 'Arsh, separated from His creation.

- **Note**: It is mentioned in the rule that "Whatever Allah and His messenger informed us we have to believe in it, whether we know its meaning or not". However, it must be acknowledged that there is nothing in the speech of Allah (سبحانه وتعالى)and His Messenger that is unknown to the whole Ummah. It must be known to the whole Ummah or at least to some of them. Allah (سبحانه وتعالى)says:

﴿...وَأَنزَلْنَا إِلَيْكَ الذِّكْرَ لِتُبَيِّنَ لِلنَّاسِ مَا نُزِّلَ إِلَيْهِمْ وَلَعَلَّهُمْ يَتَفَكَّرُونَ﴾[100]

"And We have also sent down unto you (O Muhammad) the reminder and the advice (the Qur'an), that you may explain clearly to men what is sent down to them, and that they may give thought."

And He (سبحانه وتعالى)says:

﴿...وَنَزَّلْنَا عَلَيْكَ الْكِتَابَ تِبْيَانًا لِّكُلِّ شَيْءٍ وَهُدًى وَرَحْمَةً وَبُشْرَى لِلْمُسْلِمِينَ﴾[101]

---

[100] An-Nahl: 44
[101] An-Nahl: 89

"And We have sent down to you the Book (the Qur'an) as an exposition of everything, a guidance, a mercy, and glad tidings for those who have submitted themselves (to Allah as Muslims)."

- In addition to that, If there is anything in it which no one knows of its meaning, then it would mean that certain part of Sharia'h is unknown to the Ummah. However, the issues of knowledge and unawareness are relative; something known to someone may be unknown to someone else that may be due to a deficiency in his knowledge or lack of understanding, or due to inadequacy in research or because of his bad intention.

The Third Principle

Interpreting Texts According to Their Literal Meaning

The literal meaning of the texts is the apparent meaning that comes to mind, depending on its context in the Qur'an.

It is obligatory to interpret the texts according to their literal meaning, without any misinterpretation. Allah (سبحانه وتعالى) the Highest says:

﴿وَإِنَّهُ لَتَنزِيلُ رَبِّ الْعَالَمِينَ* نَزَلَ بِهِ الرُّوحُ الأَمِينُ * عَلَى قَلْبِكَ لِتَكُونَ مِنَ الْمُنذِرِينَ * بِلِسَانٍ عَرَبِيٍّ مُّبِينٍ﴾[102]

[102] Ash-Shu'ara': 192-195.

"And truly, this (the Qur'an) is a revelation from the Lord of the 'Alamin(mankind, jinns and all that exists) * Which the trustworthy Ruh [Jibrael (Gabriel)] has brought down * Upon your heart (O Muhammad) that you may be (one) of the warners * In the plain Arabic language."

Allah (سبحانه وتعالى)says:

﴿إِنَّا جَعَلْنَاهُ قُرْآنًا عَرَبِيًّا لَّعَلَّكُمْ تَعْقِلُونَ﴾[103]

"We verily, have made it a Qur'an in Arabic, that you may be able to understand (its meanings and its admonitions)."

And Allah (سبحانه وتعالى)says:

﴿اتَّبِعُواْ مَا أُنزِلَ إِلَيْكُم مِّن رَّبِّكُمْ وَلاَ تَتَّبِعُواْ مِن دُونِهِ أَوْلِيَاء قَلِيلاً مَّا تَذَكَّرُونَ﴾[104]

"[Say (O Muhammad) to these idolaters (pagan Arabs) of your folk:] Follow what has been sent down unto you from your Lord (the Qur'an and Prophet Muhammad's Sunnah), and follow not any Auliya' (protectors and helpers, etc. who order you to associate partners in worship with Allah), besides Him (Allah). Little do you remember!"

If Allah (سبحانه وتعالى)has sent down this Qur'an in the Arabic language so that it can be understood and appreciated and commanded us to follow it, then, it becomes obligatory on us to interpret it according to its literal meaning in accordance with that Arabic language, unless it goes against a legislative truth. There is no difference between the texts that deal with the Attributes of Allah (سبحانه وتعالى) or the others. In fact, keeping to the literal meaning may be even more necessary for the texts dealing with the Attributes of Allah(سبحانه وتعالى); indeed, its context is strictly from

---

[103]Az-Zukhruf: 3
[104] Al-A'raf:3

Allah(سبحانه وتعالى), with no room for the intellect to delve into its details.

If someone says about the texts dealing with the Attributes of Allah (سبحانه وتعالى): It is not allowed to interpret the texts according to its literal meaning, because the literal meaning is not the intended one.

The answer is: What do you mean by literal meaning? Do you suggest the meanings that appear from the texts which are befitting Allah (سبحانه وتعالى), without resembling Him to the creation? If so, then this literal meaning is the intended meaning by Allah (سبحانه وتعالى) and His Messenger without a doubt; it is obligatory for the slaves to accept it, and to believe in it legally; because it is true. Additionally, it is impossible for Allah (سبحانه وتعالى) to address His slaves with a command that is contrary to the literal meaning without explaining it, while Allah (سبحانه وتعالى) says:

﴿يُرِيدُ اللَّهُ لِيُبَيِّنَ لَكُمْ وَيَهْدِيَكُمْ سُنَنَ الَّذِينَ مِن قَبْلِكُمْ...﴾[105]

"Allah (سبحانه وتعالى) wishes to make clear (what is lawful and what is unlawful) to you, and to show you the ways of those before you."

And He says:

﴿...يُبَيِّنُ اللَّهُ لَكُمْ أَن تَضِلُّواْ...﴾[106]

"(Thus) does Allah makes clear to you (His Law) lest you go astray."

Allah (سبحانه وتعالى) says about His Messenger:

---

[105] An-Nisa': 26
[106] An-Nisa': 176

﴿...وَأَنزَلْنَا إِلَيْكَ الذِّكْرَ لِتُبَيِّنَ لِلنَّاسِ مَا نُزِّلَ إِلَيْهِمْ...﴾[107]

"And We have also sent down unto you (O Muhammad) the reminder and the advice (the Qur'an), that you may explain clearly to men what is sent down to them."

And He says:

﴿...وَإِنَّكَ لَتَهْدِي إِلَى صِرَاطٍ مُّسْتَقِيمٍ﴾[108]

"And verily, you (O Muhammad) are indeed guiding (mankind) to the Straight Path i.e.

Allah(سبحانه وتعالى) 's religion of Islamic Monotheism)."

And whosoever addresses others without the apparent meaning and without explanation, then he neither explained it to him nor did he ever guide him.

Or do you suggest by literal meaning that which you perceive of resemblance? It is neither the intended meaning nor is it the literal meaning of the texts of the Qur'an and Sunnah. Such literal meaning, which you suggest is disbelief and is invalidated by the consensus of Scholars. Additionally, it is impossible for the literal meaning of the speech of Allah(سبحانه وتعالى) and His Messenger to be disbelief or invalid; indeed, no Muslim can ever agree to something like that.

The Salaf of this Ummah and its Imams have agreed that the texts dealing with the Attributes of Allah (سبحانه وتعالى) should be interpreted according to their literal meaning that is befitting Allah(سبحانه وتعالى)'s Majesty, without any misinterpretation. Additionally, keeping to the literal meaning does not necessitate resembling the Creator with the creation. Therefore, they have agreed

[107] Al-Nahl: 44
[108] Ash-Shura: 52

that Allah(سبحانه وتعالى)has Life, Knowledge, Power, Hearing, Sight, truly, and that He has actually been raised over the Heavenly Throne. Moreover, that He loves, becomes pleased, dislikes and becomes angry, truly. And that He has a Face and two Hands, truly.

As Allah(سبحانه وتعالى) the Highest says:

﴿وَتَوَكَّلْ عَلَى الْحَيِّ الَّذِي لا يَمُوتُ...﴾[109]

"And put your trust (O Muhammad) in the Ever Living One Who dies not."

And He says:

﴿...وَهُوَ بِكُلِّ شَيْءٍ عَلِيمٌ﴾[110]

"He is the All-Knower of everything."

﴿...وَهُوَ عَلَى كُلِّ شَيْءٍ قَدِيرٌ﴾[111]

"And He is Able to do all things."

He says:

﴿...وَهُوَ السَّمِيعُ الْبَصِيرُ﴾[112]

"And He is the All-Hearer, the All-Seer."

And He says:

﴿الرَّحْمَنُ عَلَى الْعَرْشِ اسْتَوَى﴾[113]

---

[109] Al-Furqan: 58
[110] Al-Baqarah: 29
[111] Al-Ma'idah: 120
[112] As-Shura:11
[113]Taha: 5

"The Most Beneficent (Allah(سبحانه وتعالى)) Istawa(rose over) the (Mighty) Throne (in a manner that suits His Majesty)."

And He says:

﴿...فَسَوْفَ يَأْتِي اللَّهُ بِقَوْمٍ يُحِبُّهُمْ وَيُحِبُّونَهُ...﴾[114]

"Allah(سبحانه وتعالى) will bring a people whom He will love and they will love Him."

And He says:

﴿...وَلَكِن كَرِهَ اللَّهُ انبِعَاثَهُمْ فَثَبَّطَهُمْ...﴾[115]

"But Allah(سبحانه وتعالى) was averse to their being sent forth, so He made them lag behind."

And He says:

﴿...وَغَضِبَ اللَّهُ عَلَيْهِ وَلَعَنَهُ...﴾[116]

"And the Wrath and the Curse of Allah are upon him."

And He says:

﴿وَيَبْقَى وَجْهُ رَبِّكَ ذُو الْجَلَالِ وَالإِكْرَامِ﴾[117]

"And the Face of your Lord full of Majesty and Honour will abide forever."

And He says:

﴿...بَلْ يَدَاهُ مَبْسُوطَتَانِ...﴾[118]

[114] Al-Ma'idah: 52
[115] At-Tawbah: 46
[116] An-Nisa': 93
[117] Ar-Rahman: 27

"Nay, both His Hands are widely outstretched."

Thus, they have interpreted these texts as well as other texts dealing with the Attributes of Allah(سبحانه وتعالى) according to their literal meaning. They have said: It is intended according to what is befitting Allah(سبحانه وتعالى)'s Majesty, without any misinterpretation or resemblance.

Explanation: Amongst our attributes are those that are semantic, such as life, knowledge, and power; while others are our parts, such as the face and the two hands. It is well known that Allah(سبحانه وتعالى)describes Himself that He is Alive, Knowledgeable and Powerful. The Muslims have never said that His Life, Knowledge and Power are similar to our life, knowledge and power. Likewise, when Allah(سبحانه وتعالى) describes Himself that He has a Face and two Hands, it does not mean that these are like our faces and hands. On the contrary, Muslims say that what is understood from the Attributes of Allah(سبحانه وتعالى), in either of these two types, does not imply the same meanings of our attributes. Rather, every attribute is relatively ascribed to the one described and is appropriate to him. Therefore, just as the Being of Allah(سبحانه وتعالى)does not resemble the beings of the creatures, likewise, His Attributes do not resemble the attributes of the creatures, as it has been previously established that the same Principle should be applied in both the Attributes and the Being.

Thus, it should be clear that: Whoever says that the literal meaning of the text is not the intended meaning, is completely in error. If he understands resemblance, from the literal meaning, his understanding is invalid and, however, if he understands not intended, his understanding stands. On the other hand, if he understands from its literal meaning the correct meaning which befits Allah(سبحانه وتعالى)'s Majesty, then he is right in his understanding but has erred in saying not intended.

[118] Al-Ma'idah: 64

Although he is right in its literal meaning, he has erred by negating it as the intended meaning, and if he has erred in its literal meaning, he is right in negating it to be the intended meaning. Therefore, his statement would have to be wrong in both measures.

The correct understanding without any errors is that its literal meaning is the intended meaning, and it is nothing but a meaning that is befitting Allah(سبحانه وتعالى).

Interpreting the Literal Meaning of the Texts incorrectly

Those who interpret the Literal Meaning of the Texts incorrectly and disapprove it; commit two errors.

- **They interpret the text erroneously, which is not indicated by the word; thereby, they disapprove it and say that the literal meaning is not the intended meaning.**

Example for this: Allah(سبحانه وتعالى) says in Hadith Qudsi: "O Children of Adam, I was ill, yet you did not visit me, O Children of Adam, I asked you for food, yet you did not feed me, O Children of Adam, I asked you for water to drink, yet you did not give me water". Hadith narrated by Muslim.[119] They say: The literal meaning of this Hadith is that Allah(سبحانه وتعالى)becomes ill, hungry and thirsty. This is an invalid meaning; therefore, it cannot be the intended meaning.

We will reply: If you interpret the text properly, it would be clear to you that this invalid meaning is not the literal meaning of the word because the context of the Hadith opposes this by further explanation. If you continue to the next part of this Hadith, where Allah(سبحانه وتعالى))

[119] Narrated by Muslim, Book of Kindness and [Family] Ties, Chapter: Visiting the Patient, no. 2569.

says: "Did you know not that so and so the person was ill, yet you did not visit him? Did you not remember that so and so person asked you for food, yet you did not feed him, and so and so person asked you for water to drink, yet you did not give him water?"[120] Here, it is clear that Allah(سبحانه وتعالى)was not ill, hungry or thirsty; in reality, it was one of His slaves that was ill, hungry and thirsty.

Another example: Allah(سبحانه وتعالى) says about Nuh's boat:

﴿تَجْرِي بِأَعْيُنِنَا...﴾[121]

"Floating under Our Eyes."

They say: The literal meaning of the verse is that the boat is floating on the eyes of Allah(سبحانه وتعالى). This is an invalid meaning; therefore, it cannot be the intended meaning.

We will reply: Your claim that the literal meaning of the verse is that the boat is floating on the eyes of Allah(سبحانه وتعالى) is rejected on the basis of sentence structure and from the contextual meaning.

According to the sentence structure: If someone says: so and so walks under my watch, nobody will understand from this syntax that the person walks on his eyes. If someone claims that this is the literal meaning, then he will be the laughing stock of the foolish people, not to mention the intellectuals. However, what is understood from this statement is that his eyes are accompanying him by watching him and by taking care of him; the preposition "ب"denotes association and not location.

[120] Part of the previous hadith.
[121] Al-Qamar: 14

According to the contextual meaning: It is known that Nuh has been on Earth, that he has crafted the boat on Earth, and that it has floated on the water on Earth. As Allah(سبحانه وتعالى) says:

﴿وَيَصْنَعُ الْفُلْكَ وَكُلَّمَا مَرَّ عَلَيْهِ مَلأٌ مِّن قَوْمِهِ سَخِرُواْ مِنْهُ...﴾[122]

"And as he was constructing the ship, whenever the chiefs of his people passed by him, they made a mockery of him."

And He says:

﴿فَدَعَا رَبَّهُ أَنِّي مَغْلُوبٌ فَانتَصِرْ * فَفَتَحْنَا أَبْوَابَ السَّمَاءِ بِمَاءٍ مُّنْهَمِرٍ * وَفَجَّرْنَا الأَرْضَ عُيُونًا فَالْتَقَى الْمَاءُ عَلَى أَمْرٍ قَدْ قُدِرَ * وَحَمَلْنَاهُ عَلَى ذَاتِ أَلْوَاحٍ وَدُسُرٍ * تَجْرِي بِأَعْيُنِنَا جَزَاءً لِّمَن كَانَ كُفِرَ﴾[123]

"Then he invoked his Lord (saying): "I have been overcome, so help (me) * So We opened the gates of heaven with water pouring forth * And We caused the earth to gush forth with springs. So the waters (of the heaven and the earth) met for a matter predestined * And We carried him on a (ship) made of planks and nails * Floating under Our Eyes, a reward for him who had been rejected!"

Nobody can claim that the literal meaning of this verse is that the boat is floating inside the Eyes of Allah(سبحانه وتعالى), because this is impossible for to be ascribed to Allah(سبحانه وتعالى).

For a person who knows Allah(سبحانه وتعالى), who exalts Him the way He should be exalted, and knows that He has been raised over His Heavenly Throne, distinct from His creations, He does not descend upon His creations nor does His creation ascend to Him, it is impossible for him to understand such an invalid meaning from these words.

---

[122] Hood: 38

[123] Al-Qamar: 10-14

Therefore, the actual meaning of this verse will be that the boat is floating under Allah(سبحانه وتعالى)'s protection.

The third example: It came in the Authentic narration that,

"الحجر الأسواد يمين الله في الأرض فمن صافحه وقبله فكأنما صافح الله وقبل يمينه"[124]

"The Black Stone is Allah(سبحانه وتعالى)'s right hand on Earth, whoever shakes or kisses it, it is as if he has shaken or has kissed

Allah(سبحانه وتعالى)'s right hand."

They say: The literal meaning of this Hadith is that the Black Stone itself is Allah(سبحانه وتعالى)'s right hand on Earth; this is an invalid meaning; therefore, it is not the intended meaning.

We will say: Firstly: This Hadith has not been authentically narrated on behalf of the Prophet ﷺ, but the famous opinion is that it is saying of Ibn Abbâs.

I say [my opinion is that]: Ibn Jawzi says: This Hadith is not authentic; Ibn al-'Arabi says: This is a fabricated Hadith; it should not be considered.

Secondly: If we accept it as an authentic Hadith, it is clear to everyone that the Black Stone itself is not Allah(سبحانه وتعالى)'s Right hand because he says: "Right hand on Earth." Thus, this restricted meaning contravenes the general meaning. Additionally, it is well known that Allah(سبحانه وتعالى)is in Heaven. Also, he says: "whoever shakes or kisses it, it is as if he has shaken or kissed Allah(سبحانه وتعالى)'s Right Hand;" we know that two similar things do not share a common similarity. Therefore, it is clear from this narration that whoever touches

[124] Ibn 'Adi narrated in al-Kamil, (1/336), Ibn al-Jawzi in al-'Ilal al-Mutanahiyah, (2/84,85), al-'Ajluni in Kashf al-Khafa (1109), and al-Albanisaid in his as-Silsilah ad-Da'eefah (223): "This hadith is *Munkar*."

the Black Stone has not really shaken Allah(سبحانه وتعالى)'s Hand, and that the Black Stone itself is not the right Hand of Allah(سبحانه وتعالى). So, how could this apparent meaning be considered disbelief that needs to be reinterpreted?

- **They interpret the text correctly according to its literal meaning; however, they reject it because they think it is a false meaning although it is the correct one.**

Example of this: Allah(سبحانه وتعالى)says:

﴿الرَّحْمَنُ عَلَى الْعَرْشِ اسْتَوَى﴾[125]

"The Most Beneficent (Allah) Istawa(rose over) the (Mighty) Throne (in a manner that suits His Majesty)."

They say: the literal meaning of this verse is that Allah(سبحانه وتعالى) is on the Heavenly Throne. The Heavenly Throne is limited which would necessitate for Allah(سبحانه وتعالى) to be limited as well; therefore, this is an invalid meaning and therefore it is not the intended meaning.

We will say: Allah(سبحانه وتعالى)'s rising over His Heavenly Throne– even if the Heavenly Throne is limited – does not necessitate a false or incorrect meaning.

Indeed, Allah(سبحانه وتعالى) has been raised over the Heavenly Throne in a manner that is befitting His Majesty and in a manner that does not resemble the rising of a creation over another creation. Also, it does not necessitate for Allah(سبحانه وتعالى) to be limited; it is an elevation that is specific to the Throne, and Throne is the highest creation; thus, Allah(سبحانه وتعالى)will be above all everything. And such is due to His perfection and perfection of His Attributes. So, how could it be an invalid meaning or not the intended meaning?!

---

[125]Taha: 5

Another example: Allah(سبحانه وتعالى) says:

﴿...بَلْ يَدَاهُ مَبْسُوطَتَانِ يُنفِقُ كَيْفَ يَشَاءُ...﴾[126]

"Nay, both His Hands are widely outstretched. He spends (of His Bounty) as He wills."

They say: The literal meaning of this verse indicates that Allah(سبحانه وتعالى) has two real Hands, which are organs. This is an invalid meaning and thus it is not the intended meaning.

We will say: Affirming two real hands for Allah(سبحانه وتعالى) does not necessitate an invalid meaning; indeed, Allah(سبحانه وتعالى) has two real Hands, which are befitting His Majesty; with these Hands, He takes and seizes. However, these Hands do not resemble the hands of the creation. And such is due to His perfection and perfection of His Attributes. Allah(سبحانه وتعالى) says:

﴿وَمَا قَدَرُوا اللَّهَ حَقَّ قَدْرِهِ وَالأَرْضُ جَمِيعًا قَبْضَتُهُ يَوْمَ الْقِيَامَةِ وَالسَّمَاوَاتُ مَطْوِيَّاتٌ بِيَمِينِهِ...﴾[127]

"They made not a just estimate of Allah such as is due to Him. And on the Day of Resurrection, the whole of the earth will be grasped by His Hand and the heavens will be rolled up in His Right Hand."

In Sahih Muslim, it has been narrated by Abu Hurayrah ﷺ that the Prophet ﷺ says:

"ما تصدق أحد بصدقة من طيب – ولا يقبل الله إلا الطيب – إلا أخذها الرحمن بيمينه وإن كانت تمرة فتربو في كف الرحمن حتى تكون أعظم من الجبل"[128]

[126] Al-Ma'idah: 64
[127] Az-Zumar: 67
[128] Al-Bukhari: Book of Charity; Chapter: Charity from the lawfully earned, (1410); Muslim: Book of Charity; Chapter: Acceptance of Charity from the lawfully earned, (1014).

"Whoever gives charity that is earned in a lawful way, and Allah(سبحانه وتعالى) only accepts what is lawful, Allah(سبحانه وتعالى) shall take it in His right Hand, if it is dated, it grows in the Hand of Allah(سبحانه وتعالى), the Merciful, so much so that it becomes as big as a mountain".

What invalid meaning is necessitated from the literal meaning of the text, then, that they should say it is thus not intended?!

The fault appears twice in one example like the Prophet ﷺ's saying:

"إن قلوب بني آدم كلها بين إصبعين من أصابع الرحمن كقلب واحد يصرفه حيث يشاء"[129]

"All the hearts of the children of Adam are between Allah(سبحانه وتعالى)'s Fingers as if it is one heart; He can turn it as He wishes."

They say according to the first perspective: The literal meaning of this Hadith tells us that the hearts of the children of Adam are between Allah(سبحانه وتعالى)'s Fingers, which would necessitate direct contact and touch, and that Allah(سبحانه وتعالى)'s Fingers should be inside of us. Therefore, this meaning is invalid; thus, it cannot be intended.

They say according to the second perspective: The literal meaning of this Hadith tells us that Allah(سبحانه وتعالى) has real Fingers, and fingers are organs; therefore, this is an invalid meaning and thus is not intended.

We will reply to the first perspective by saying: The fact that the hearts of the children of Adam are between

Allah(سبحانه وتعالى)'s two Fingers does not necessitate from Him direct contact and touch, neither does it necessitate for Allah(سبحانه وتعالى)'s

[129] Muslim: Book of Qadar; Chapter: Changing the Heartas Allah Wishes, No. 2654.

Fingers to be inside of us. Have you not seen that Allah(سبحانه وتعالى) says:

﴿...وَالسَّحَابِ الْمُسَخَّرِ بَيْنَ السَّمَاء وَالأَرْضِ...﴾[130]

"And clouds which are held between the sky and the earth."

Here, the clouds touch neither the heaven nor the earth directly.

As it is also said: "سترة المصلى بين يديه" Shield of the one praying is before him; it is neither in direct contact nor is it touching him.

If the between-ness does not necessitate direct contact and touch among the creation, then how about the between-ness, between the creation and the Creator, whose footstool or chair extends over the heavens and the earth and that He encompasses all things. It is has been proven by both text and intellect that Allah(سبحانه وتعالى)is distinctive from His creation and that He does not merge within the creation nor does the creations merge within Him, and the Salafs have agreed upon this issue.

We will reply to the second perspective by saying: Affirming the fingers for Allah(سبحانه وتعالى) does not necessitate an invalid meaning, and thus it would definitely be the intended meaning. Indeed, Allah(سبحانه وتعالى) has fingers which are befitting His majesty and that do not resemble the fingers of the creation. It is mentioned in Sahih Al-Bukhari and Muslim, on the authority of Ibn Mas'ud ﷺ that he says: A rabbi came to Allah(سبحانه وتعالى)'s Messenger ﷺ and said: "Oh, Muhammad! We are told that Allah(سبحانه وتعالى) will put all the heavens on one Finger and the Earths on one Finger and the trees on one Finger and the water and the dust on one Finger and all the other created beings on one Finger. Then He will say: 'I am the King.'

[130] Al-Baqarah: 164

Thereupon, the Prophet ﷺ laughed until his molar teeth were visible and this was a confirmation of the rabbi's words. Then he ﷺ recited:

﴿وَمَا قَدَرُوا اللَّهَ حَقَّ قَدْرِهِ وَالأَرْضُ جَمِيعًا قَبْضَتُهُ يَوْمَ الْقِيَامَةِ وَالسَّمَاوَاتُ مَطْوِيَّاتٌ بِيَمِينِهِ سُبْحَانَهُ وَتَعَالَى عَمَّا يُشْرِكُونَ﴾[131]

"They made not a just estimate of Allah such as is due to Him. And on the Day of Resurrection, the whole of the earth will be grasped by His Hand and the heavens will be rolled up in His Right Hand. Glorified is He, and High is He above all that they associate as partners with Him!"

This part has been taken from the Bukhari's commentary on Surah al-Zumar. So what invalid meaning is then necessitated from the literal meaning of the text that so that it is said that it is not intended?!

This mistake is like making a word comparable to that which is not similar to it, as it has been said about the verse:

﴿...لِمَا خَلَقْتُ بِيَدَيَّ...﴾[132]

"Whom I have created with Both My Hands."

That it is like the verse:

﴿...مِمَّا عَمِلَتْ أَيْدِينَا...﴾[133]

"What Our Hands have created."

The claim would be that since the hand is a 'subject' in both verses, then the intended meaning is the same. This is incorrect because the difference between them can be proven from three perspectives:

[131] Az-Zumar: 67
[132] Sad: 75
[133] Yasin: 71

- From the structural perspective, Allah(سبحانه وتعالى) says in the first verse, ﴿...لِمَا خَلَقْتُ بِيَدَيَّ...﴾, this syntax is different from the one in the second verse, where Allah(سبحانه وتعالى)says:

﴿...مِمَّا عَمِلَتْ أَيْدِينَا...﴾ . If the first verse is similar to the second one, it would have said "لما خلقت يداي", whereupon the act of creation would have been an object of the hands just as the action is an object of the hands in the second verse.

- In the first verse, Allah(سبحانه وتعالى)refers the action to Himself; it is by the use of His hands. So Allah(سبحانه وتعالى) is the Creator and He created it with His hands. See you not the statement of the one who says: "كتبت بالقلم" "I wrote with the pen"; here the writer is the author of the writing, and the 'ب'came in-between to show that the writing has been done with the pen.

On the other hand, in the second verse, ﴿...مِمَّا عَمِلَتْ أَيْدِينَا...﴾ here the action refers to the hands and hands refer to Him; referring the action to the hands is like referring the action to Himself. It is as if he says: Which we have done. See you not that He says:

﴿وَمَا أَصَابَكُم مِّن مُّصِيبَةٍ فَبِمَا كَسَبَتْ أَيْدِيكُمْ...﴾[134]

"And whatever of misfortune befalls you, it is because of what your hands have earned."

The intended meaning here is 'because of what you have earned', as proven by another verse:

﴿فَأَصَابَهُمْ سَيِّئَاتُ مَا كَسَبُوا...﴾[135]

[134] Ash-Shura: 30
[135]Az-Zumar: 51

"So, the evil results of that which they earned overtook them."

- Allah(سبحانه وتعالى)refers to the action in the first verse, ﴿...لِمَا خَلَقْتُ بِيَدَيَّ...﴾to two hands through the usage of "ب". It is impossible that He meant by these two Himself because the number **two** only means a count of two, and Allah(سبحانه وتعالى) is only **One**. Therefore, it is impossible that He refers to Himself with the **two** because **two** clearly refers to a count of **two**, as we have said.

However, Allah(سبحانه وتعالى) may sometimes use the singular form to refer to Himself to indicate Tawheed, and sometimes the plural form 'We' to indicate His Majesty. Perhaps the plural form is indicative of the meanings of His names.

As for the second verse, the action refers to the hands, which refer to Him, in the plural form to indicate His Majesty. Therefore, they are actually referring to His Majestic Self.

Thus, the difference between these two verses:﴿...لِمَا خَلَقْتُ بِيَدَيَّ...﴾ and ﴿...مِمَّا عَمِلَتْ أَيْدِينَا...﴾should have been clarified; that the first verse is not similar to the second verse. It should also be clear that the literal meaning of the texts mentioning the Attributes is an established truth that should be done in a manner befitting Allah(سبحانه وتعالى)'s Majesty. Additionally, [the usage of the literal meaning], neither imposes any deficiencies on His part nor does it resemble Him to the creation.

But when we talk to a person who is not able to understand the literal meaning without falling in resemblance, we shall tell him: The literal meaning which you have understood is not the intended meaning. Then, we shall explain to him that this is not the literal meaning of the text because it is a false meaning uncalled for according to the context, as we have discussed previously.

The Fourth Principle

The assumption of some people about the texts mentioning the Attributes of Allah(سبحانه وتعالى) and the dangers in it.

Know that many people assume about some of the Attributes, as has been indicated by the texts, or any of it or most of it, or even all of it that they resemble the attributes of the creatures. Then, he wishes to negate this assumption; thereby, he falls into four dangers:

- ✓ He understands from the texts that the attributes of Allah (سبحانه وتعالى) resemble the attributes of the creatures, and he assumes that this is the intended meaning of the text. This is an incorrect understanding because the attributes that are indicated in the text are only appropriate and suitable to the one described.

Resembling the Creator with the creatures is considered disbelief and misguidance. This is because it is a renunciation of Allah(سبحانه وتعالى)'s saying:

﴿...لَيْسَ كَمِثْلِهِ شَيْءٌ...﴾[136]

"There is nothing like unto Him."

And it is impossible that the literal meaning of the texts is disbelief and misguidance. Allah(سبحانه وتعالى) says:

﴿يُرِيدُ اللَّهُ لِيُبَيِّنَ لَكُمْ وَيَهْدِيَكُمْ سُنَنَ الَّذِينَ مِن قَبْلِكُمْ...﴾[137]

[136] Ash-Shura: 11
[137] An-Nisa': 26

"Allah(سبحانه وتعالى) wishes to make clear (what is lawful and what is unlawful) to you, and to show you the ways of those before you."

Allah(سبحانه وتعالى) says:

﴿...يُبَيِّنُ اللَّهُ لَكُمْ أَن تَضِلُّواْ...﴾[138]

"(Thus) does Allah make clear to you (His Law) lest you go astray."

- ✓ He has been unjust to the texts; he negates the divine meanings, which are indicated by the texts, then he affirms other fabricated meanings for it, which are not signified by the text. Therefore, he has done injustice to the texts from two angles.
- ✓ He denies the Attributes that are indicated by the texts without knowledge; as a result, he speaks about Allah(سبحانه وتعالى) with no knowledge. This is prohibited according to the texts and scholarly consensus.

Allah(سبحانه وتعالى) says:

﴿قُلْ إِنَّمَا حَرَّمَ رَبِّيَ الْفَوَاحِشَ مَا ظَهَرَ مِنْهَا وَمَا بَطَنَ وَالإِثْمَ وَالْبَغْيَ بِغَيْرِ الْحَقِّ وَأَن تُشْرِكُواْ بِاللَّهِ مَا لَمْ يُنَزِّلْ بِهِ سُلْطَانًا وَأَن تَقُولُواْ عَلَى اللَّهِ مَا لاَ تَعْلَمُونَ﴾[139]

"Say (O Muhammadﷺ): '(But) the things that my Lord has indeed forbidden are Al-Fawahish(great evil sins, every kind of unlawful sexual intercourse, etc.) whether committed openly or secretly, sins (of all kinds), unrighteous oppression, joining partners (in worship) with Allah for which He has given no authority, and saying things about Allah of which you have no knowledge.'"

- ✓ Whenever he negates the Attributes of perfection as indicated by the texts, then it will necessitate for Allah(سبحانه وتعالى)to be characterized with its opposite, which are characteristics of

[138] An-Nisa': 176
[139] Al-A'raf: 33

imperfection. It is because nothing exists except that it has characteristics. It is impossible for a being to exist void of characteristics. Therefore, if it is not characterized by the characteristics of perfection, then it must be characterized by the characteristics of imperfection.

Therefore, whoever negates the attributes of perfection of Allah(سبحانه وتعالى), as indicated by the texts, then he has transgressed against Allah(سبحانه وتعالى); indeed, he has combined between negating Allah(سبحانه وتعالى)'s Attributes of perfection and resembling Him with the imperfect and non-existing beings. Nay, he may even go so far in negation that he resembles Him with beings that are impossible to come into existence.

Therefore, he would be doing injustice to the texts as well. This is because he suspends its implied meanings of Allah(سبحانه وتعالى)'s perfect attributes, and then he affirms fabricated meanings, which are not implied by its literal meaning. Thus, he combines between negating and resembling Allah(سبحانه وتعالى)'s Attributes; and between corrupting and suspending the texts of the Qur'an and Sunnah. Thereby, he disbelieves in the names of Allah(سبحانه وتعالى) and His verses.

Allah(سبحانه وتعالى) says about this:

﴿وَلِلَّهِ الأَسْمَاء الْحُسْنَى فَادْعُوهُ بِهَا وَذَرُواْ الَّذِينَ يُلْحِدُونَ فِي أَسْمَائِهِ سَيُجْزَوْنَ مَا كَانُواْ يَعْمَلُونَ﴾[140]

"And (all) the Most Beautiful Names belong to Allah, so call on Him by them, and leave the company of those who belie or deny (or utter impious speech against) His Names. They will be requited for what they used to do."

[140] Al-A'raf: 180

﴿إِنَّ الَّذِينَ يُلْحِدُونَ فِي آيَاتِنَا لا يَخْفَوْنَ عَلَيْنَا أَفَمَن يُلْقَى فِي النَّارِ خَيْرٌ أَم مَّن يَأْتِي آمِنًا يَوْمَ الْقِيَامَةِ اعْمَلُوا مَا شِئْتُمْ إِنَّهُ بِمَا تَعْمَلُونَ بَصِيرٌ﴾[141]

"Verily, those who turn away from Our Ayat (proofs, evidence, verses, lessons, signs, revelations, etc. by attacking, distorting and denying them), are not hidden from Us. Is he who is cast into the Fire better or he who comes secure on the Day of Resurrection? Do what you will. Verily! He is All-Seer of what you do (this is a severe threat to the disbelievers)."

Example: Allah(سبحانه وتعالى) informs us about Himself that He has been raised over the Throne. Someone may then assume that His rising over the Throne is like the rising of the people on a ship or a livestock and that Allah(سبحانه وتعالى) needs the Throne just as people need livestock and ship. If the livestock tumbles then the person who rides on it will fall down; if the ship sinks into the water then those riding on it will sink as well. According to this false analogy, if the Throne disappears, then Allah(سبحانه وتعالى) will fall down! And therefore, they negate the reality of the Istiwa [rising over]. The reason behind this assumption is that they liken the rising of Allah(سبحانه وتعالى) on the Throne with the rising of people on livestock or a ship. This is a false analogy because Allah(سبحانه وتعالى)ascribes the rising to His Honorable Self; neither does He ever mention any type of rising that may be appropriate for the creation nor does He generalize it to include the creation as well. Therefore, this specification indicates that this rising is special only for Allah (سبحانه وتعالى) that is appropriate for Him, just like the rest of His attributes and actions. His rising Istiwâ does not resemble the Istiwâ of the creation just as Allah (سبحانه وتعالى) does not resemble the creation.

Allah(سبحانه وتعالى)says:

---

[141]Fussilat: 40

﴿وَالسَّمَاءَ بَنَيْنَاهَا بِأَيْدٍ...﴾[142]

"With power did We construct the heaven."

Would anybody ever assume that the construction of the heaven is like the construction of the roof for someone's house; whereupon he would need frail, shovels, bricks, and clay to build it? If Allah(سبحانه وتعالى) does not need these things for this action, then He needs not the Throne to rise upon it. Indeed, Allah(سبحانه وتعالى)needs neither the Throne nor any other things; [He is the Self-Sufficient].

Consequently, as this person negates the actual Istiwâ, which is what is apparent from the texts, he falls into four dangers:

1. He resembles the Istiwâ of Allah(سبحانه وتعالى), as he understands it, with the Istiwâ of the creation.
2. He suspends the texts regarding Allah(سبحانه وتعالى)'s Istiwâ, which is appropriate with Allah (سبحانه وتعالى)'s Majesty; thereafter, he alters it to denote other meanings, which are not otherwise implied.
3. His negation and suspension are without knowledge; indeed, it is based on ignorance and false assumption.
4. By negating the attribute of perfection in Istiwâ, necessitates affirming an imperfect attribute.

Another example: Allah(سبحانه وتعالى) says:

﴿أَأَمِنتُم مَّن فِي السَّمَاءِ أَن يَخْسِفَ بِكُمُ الأَرْضَ فَإِذَا هِيَ تَمُورُ﴾[143]

"Do you feel secure that He, Who is over the heaven (Allah), will not cause the earth to sink with you, then behold it shakes (as in an earthquake)?"

---

[142] Adh-Dhariyat: 47
[143] Al-Mulk: 16

Some people may be deluded to think that Allah(سبحانه وتعالى)is inside the heaven and that it is surrounding Him, just as if we say, so and so is inside the room because the room surrounds him. Based on this assumption, they negate the fact that Allah(سبحانه وتعالى)is over the heaven; instead, they claim that what in the heaven is actually His kingdom, His power and so on.

The source of this assumption is that they assume that the proposition"في" has only one meaning, wherever it may be. This is a false assumption because "في" has several meanings based on the word that is attached to it. There is a difference between a 'thing inside a place', or being 'displayed on a body', or for 'the face to be on a mirror', and for 'the words to be written on a paper'. If someone says: 'Is the Throne in the heaven or in the earth?' It will be said to him, 'It is in heaven', although the Throne is much bigger than heaven.

Based on this, in this statement ﴿أَأَمِنتُم مَّن فِي السَّمَاءِ﴾ has two meanings: Either, heaven means highness, because sometimes [heaven or sky] is used to indicate highness, as in Allah(سبحانه وتعالى)'s saying:

﴿...وَأَنزَلَ لَكُم مِّنَ السَّمَاءِ مَاءً...﴾[144]

"And sends down for you water (rain) from the sky."

We know that the rain comes down from the clouds, which are between the sky and the earth, not from the sky itself. Likewise, the fact that Allah(سبحانه وتعالى) is in heaven means that He is the absolute high, above all creations; nothing can surround Him, because there is nothing above the world except Allah(سبحانه وتعالى). Or it means, 'on,' where this meaning is derived from Allah(سبحانه وتعالى)'s saying:

﴿...فَسِيرُواْ فِي الأَرْضِ...﴾[145]

[144] An-Naml: 60

"So travel through the earth."

It means 'on the earth'. Allah(سبحانه وتعالى) also says about Firaun:

﴿...وَلَأُصَلِّبَنَّكُمْ فِي جُذُوعِ النَّخْلِ...﴾[146]

"I will surely crucify you on the trunks of date-palms."

Here also, the proposition"في" means 'on'. Therefore, according to this, the meaning of the Allah(سبحانه وتعالى)'s saying:﴿أَأَمِنتُم مَّن فِي السَّمَاءِ﴾ will be 'On the heaven, above it'; Allah(سبحانه وتعالى)is on the heaven, above everything.

Consequently, as this person negates that Allah(سبحانه وتعالى) is literally in the heavens, which is what is apparent from the texts, he falls into four dangers:

1. He resembles the fact that Allah(سبحانه وتعالى) being on the heaven, as he understands it, with a creature being in the room and so on.
2. He suspends the texts and what they indicate of Allah

(سبحانه وتعالى)'s highness above heaven; thereafter, he alters them to denote other meanings, which are not otherwise implied.

3. His negation and suspension are without knowledge; indeed, it is based on ignorance and false assumption.
4. By negating the attribute of perfection in Him being in the heaven, necessitates affirming an imperfect attribute. Indeed, negating the attribute of highness must necessitate one of two things:

Either Allah(سبحانه وتعالى)exists everywhere with His being; however, this is great disbelief and misguidance because it necessitates either the plurality of the creator or the divisibility of the creator. Likewise, it

---

[145] Ali 'Imran: 137
[146]Taha: 71

necessitates for Him to exist in dirty places, which no honorable person wants to go to, let alone the Creator.

Or that Allah(سبحانه وتعالى) the Highest should neither exist inside the world nor outside of it; neither above it nor below it; neither attached to it nor separated from it; neither distinct not merged to it, and so on with similar phrases which indicate absolute suspension. This is actually negating the existence of Allah(سبحانه وتعالى)'s Being.

The Fifth Principle

Our Knowledge about What Allah(سبحانه وتعالى) Informed us About Himself

What Allah(سبحانه وتعالى) has informed us about Himself is known to us from one perspective of meaning, yet unknown to us in its manner of being (i.e. how it is).

As for it being known to us from the perspective of meaning, it is established by textual and intellectual proofs.

The Textual Proofs: Allah(سبحانه وتعالى) says:

﴿كِتَابٌ أَنزَلْنَاهُ إِلَيْكَ مُبَارَكٌ لِّيَدَّبَّرُوا آيَاتِهِ وَلِيَتَذَكَّرَ أُوْلُوا الأَلْبَابِ﴾[147]

"(This is) a Book (the Qur'an) which We have sent down to you, full of blessings that they may ponder over its Verses, and that men of understanding may remember."

And He says:

[147] Sad: 29

﴿أَفَلاَ يَتَدَبَّرُونَ الْقُرْآنَ وَلَوْ كَانَ مِنْ عِندِ غَيْرِ اللَّهِ لَوَجَدُواْ فِيهِ اخْتِلافًا كَثِيرًا﴾[148]

"Do they not then consider the Qur'an carefully? Had it been from other than Allah, they would surely have found there in many contradictions."

﴿أَفَلا يَتَدَبَّرُونَ الْقُرْآنَ أَمْ عَلَى قُلُوبٍ أَقْفَالُهَا﴾[149]

"Do they not then think deeply in the Qur'an, or are their hearts locked up (from understanding it)?

The Prophet ﷺ says:

"خيركم من تعلم القرآن وعلمه"[150]

"The best among you is who learns the Qur'an and teaches other."

Allah(سبحانه وتعالى) encourages us to ponder over the whole Qur'an with no exception. And He rebukes those who do not ponder upon it. He explains that the wisdom behind sending down the Qur'an is for those, whom the Qur'an has been sent down, to ponder over it, and for those with a sound intellect to take heed. If there is no meaning that may be derived through pondering, then the encouragement to ponder it would be nonsensical. Additionally, busying oneself with pondering it would be a waste of time. And so, the wisdom behind sending it down would cease to exist, and rebuking those who neglect it would not be appropriate.

The encouragement for pondering the Qur'an encompasses all its informational as well as wisdom-based verses. We are commanded to ponder the legislative verses to understand its meanings and act

148 An-Nisa': 82
149 Muhammad: 24
150 Al-Bukhari, Book: The Virtue of the Qur'an; Chapter: The best among you is someone who learns the Qur'an and teaches it.

accordingly because it is impossible to act upon it without understanding. Likewise, we are commanded to ponder the informational verses to understand their meanings and believe accordingly, glorifying Allah(سبحانه وتعالى) with them, because it is impossible to believe that which we do not understand or to glorify Allah(سبحانه وتعالى) with it.

The intellectual proofs about understanding the meanings of Allah(سبحانه وتعالى)'s information about Himself, it is from two perspectives:

Firstly: Allah(سبحانه وتعالى)'s information about Himself is the highest and best category of information. It is impossible for the meaning of the information that Allah(سبحانه وتعالى) gives about Himself to be unknown; while, the meaning of the information about Pharaoh, Haman, Qarun, the people of Nuh, 'Âd, Thamud, and those who have come after them is known. The creation's necessity of understanding the meaning of the information given by Allah(سبحانه وتعالى) about Himself is rather obvious and more pertinent.

Secondly: It is impossible that Allah(سبحانه وتعالى) sends down a Book to His slaves, wherein He introduces to them His Names, Attributes, Actions, and Legislations and describes Himself as the Most High, Most Wise[151], Most Generous[152], Most Great[153] and All-Glorious[154] in the clear Arabic language so it can be reasoned and understood;[155]yet, His words

---

151﴿وَإِنَّهُ فِي أُمِّ الْكِتَابِ لَدَيْنَا لَعَلِيٌّ حَكِيمٌ﴾

152﴿إِنَّهُ لَقُرْآنٌ كَرِيمٌ﴾

153﴿وَلَقَدْ آتَيْنَاكَ سَبْعًا مِّنَ الْمَثَانِي وَالْقُرْآنَ الْعَظِيمَ﴾

154﴿بَلْ هُوَ قُرْآنٌ مَّجِيدٌ﴾

155 ﴿حم * وَالْكِتَابِ الْمُبِينِ * إِنَّا جَعَلْنَاهُ قُرْآنًا عَرَبِيًّا لَّعَلَّكُمْ تَعْقِلُونَ﴾

regarding the best of pursuits be unknown, just like the alphabets, which no one knows about its meaning, except for worthless conjectures that leaves them but ignorant. As Allah(سبحانه وتعالى) says:

﴿وَمِنْهُمْ أُمِّيُّونَ لاَ يَعْلَمُونَ الْكِتَابَ إِلاَّ أَمَانِيَّ...﴾[156]

"And there are among them (Jews) unlettered people, who know not the Book, but they trust upon false desires and they but guess."

If you say: How then do you answer to Allah(سبحانه وتعالى)'s saying:

﴿هُوَ الَّذِيَ أَنزَلَ عَلَيْكَ الْكِتَابَ مِنْهُ آيَاتٌ مُّحْكَمَاتٌ هُنَّ أُمُّ الْكِتَابِ وَأُخَرُ مُتَشَابِهَاتٌ فَأَمَّا الَّذِينَ فِي قُلُوبِهِمْ زَيْغٌ فَيَتَّبِعُونَ مَا تَشَابَهَ مِنْهُ ابْتِغَاء الْفِتْنَةِ وَابْتِغَاء تَأْوِيلِهِ وَمَا يَعْلَمُ تَأْوِيلَهُ إِلاَّ اللّهُ وَالرَّاسِخُونَ فِي الْعِلْمِ يَقُولُونَ آمَنَّا بِهِ كُلٌّ مِّنْ عِندِ رَبِّنَا وَمَا يَذَّكَّرُ إِلاَّ أُوْلُواْ الألْبَابِ﴾[157]

"It is He Who has sent down to you (Muhammad) the Book (this Qur'an). In it are Verses that are entirely clear, they are the foundations of the Book [and those are the Verses of Al-Ahkam(commandments, etc.), Al-Fara'id(obligatory duties) and Al-Hudud(legal laws for the punishment of thieves, adulterers, etc.)]; and others not entirely clear. So as for those in whose hearts there is a deviation (from the truth) they follow that which is not entirely clear thereof, seeking Al-Fitnah (polytheism and trials, etc.), and seeking for its hidden meanings, but none knows its hidden meanings save Allah. And those who are firmly grounded in knowledge say: 'We believe in it; the whole of it (clear and unclear Verses) are from our Lord.' And none receives admonition except men of understanding. (Tafsir At-Tabari)."

This verse would necessitate that there are some verses in the Qur'an with hidden meanings, which are not entirely clear, that nobody knows except Allah(سبحانه وتعالى)?

[156] Al-Baqarah: 78
[157] Al-Imran: 7

We will say: There are two opinions among the early scholars about this verse:

- To stop the recitation at﴿إِلاَّ اللَّهُ﴾ [except

Allah(سبحانه وتعالى)], this is the opinion of the majority of the early and late scholars. Based on this, the intended interpretation (but none knows its hidden meanings save Allah(سبحانه وتعالى)) is the real interpretation of the sentence, not the commentary in explanation of the meaning. Likewise, explaining the verses, which refer to the attributes of Allah(سبحانه وتعالى), in this manner is the reality of these attributes and their essence. This issue is from the issues of the unseen that no intellect can grasp and no revealed texts mention it; therefore, nobody knows it except Allah(سبحانه وتعالى).

- To continue the recitation without stopping after

﴿إِلاَّ اللَّهُ﴾,this is the opinion of a group from the early and late scholars. Based on this, the intended interpretation(but none knows its hidden meanings save Allah(سبحانه وتعالى)) will be the exegesis in explaining the meaning. This explanation is known to those scholars who are firmly grounded in knowledge, Ibn 'Abbas ﷺ says: "I'm one of those who are firmly grounded in its interpretation". Mujahid says: "I went over the Mushaf with Ibn 'Abbas from its Fatiha until the end and I would stop on each verse asking him about it".

Thus, it becomes clear to us that the abovementioned verse does not indicate that there are unknown things in the Qur'an, which nobody knows their meaning except Allah(سبحانه وتعالى). Conversely, it indicates that there are some verses in the Qur'an whose reality and essence cannot be known except by Allah(سبحانه وتعالى), according to the first opinion. And according to the second opinion, it indicates that the firmly-grounded scholars know the meanings of the "unclear verses"

[المتشابة], whose meaning may be unknown to the majority of the people. Therefore, there is no contradiction in what we have mentioned previously, that there is nothing in the Qur'an whose meaning is unknown.

The Matter of Being is Unknown

As for what Allah(سبحانه وتعالى)has informed us about Himself, its matter of being is unknown; yet, it is affirmed by textual and intellectual proofs.

Textual Evidence, from two angles:

- Allah(سبحانه وتعالى) the Highest says:

﴿يَعْلَمُ مَا بَيْنَ أَيْدِيهِمْ وَمَا خَلْفَهُمْ وَلا يُحِيطُونَ بِهِ عِلْمًا﴾[158]

"He (Allah(سبحانه وتعالى)) knows what happens to them (His creatures) in this world, and what will happen to them (in the Hereafter), and they will never compass anything of His Knowledge."

Indeed, to negate the ability to compass anything of His knowledge also includes compassing His Self as well as His attributes. Nobody truly knows His Self nor its Essence except Him; and the same for His attributes.

- Indeed, Allah(سبحانه وتعالى)has informed us about Himself and His Attributes but He has not informed us about their matter of being [The How]. Our minds cannot grasp its reality; therefore, its matter of being is unknown to us. It is therefore

[158]Taha: 110

impermissible for us to speak about it or to assess it with our minds. Allah(سبحانه وتعالى) the Highest says:

﴿وَلاَ تَقْفُ مَا لَيْسَ لَكَ بِهِ عِلْمٌ إِنَّ السَّمْعَ وَالْبَصَرَ وَالْفُؤَادَ كُلُّ أُوْلَئِكَ كَانَ عَنْهُ مَسْؤُولاً﴾[159]

"And follow not (O man i.e., say not, or do not or witness not, etc.) that of which you have no knowledge (e.g. one's saying: 'I have seen,' while in fact he has not seen, or 'I have heard,' while he has not heard). Verily! The hearing, and the sight, and the heart, of each of those you will be questioned (by Allah)."

﴿قُلْ إِنَّمَا حَرَّمَ رَبِّيَ الْفَوَاحِشَ مَا ظَهَرَ مِنْهَا وَمَا بَطَنَ وَالإِثْمَ وَالْبَغْيَ بِغَيْرِ الْحَقِّ وَأَن تُشْرِكُواْ بِاللَّهِ مَا لَمْ يُنَزِّلْ بِهِ سُلْطَانًا وَأَن تَقُولُواْ عَلَى اللَّهِ مَا لاَ تَعْلَمُونَ﴾[160]

"Say (O Muhammad): '(But) the things that my Lord has indeed forbidden are Al-Fawahish(great evil sins, every kind of unlawful sexual intercourse, etc.) whether committed openly or secretly, sins (of all kinds), unrighteous oppression, joining partners (in worship) with Allah for which He has given no authority, and saying things about Allah of which you have no knowledge.'"

Intellectual Evidence: Nothing can be known perfectly except by either observing it or observing something comparable to it, or through authentic information about it. However, none of these media exists regarding the matter of being for Allah(سبحانه وتعالى)'s Self and His attributes. Therefore, the matter of being of Allah(سبحانه وتعالى)'s Self and His Attributes are unknown to us.

Additionally, we say: How will you assess Allah(سبحانه وتعالى)'s Self and His attributes? Indeed, any assumption you may conjure up in your mind or speak about it by your tongue, Allah(سبحانه وتعالى)is greater than that. And any assumption you may conjure up in your mind or

[159] Al-Isra': 36
[160] Al-A'raf: 33

speak about it by your tongue will be considered a lie because there is no evidence for it.

Conclusion

As per the report, it was clear that it is impossible for the Qur'an to contain something unknown except to Allah(سبحانه وتعالى). Thus, the invalidity of those who pass over the meanings of the verses on the attributes, and even attribute it to the methodology of the Salaf is clear. Indeed, they have erred in their claim and lied in saying it is the way of the Salaf. The Salaf only passes over the issue of the matter of being [the how], not the issue of the meaning. It has been authentically narrated on numerous occasions their affirmation of meanings of the texts, sometimes discussed briefly and other times extensively. An example of a brief discussion is his saying: "Take it as it appears without asking how."[161] An example of the extensive discussion is what has been previously mentioned regarding the statement of [Imam] Malik on Istiwâ.

Shaykh al-Islam Ibn Taymiyah mentions in his book,

"درء تعارض العقل والنقل"[Fending Off Contradictions Between the Intellect and Revealed Texts]; also known as"العقل والنقل"[The Intellect and the Revealed Texts] (1/16), which is published as an annotation of Minhaj As-Sunnah (1/201) edited by Rashad Salim; "As for passing over the meaning [التفويض], it is well known that Allah(سبحانه وتعالى) commands us to ponder over the Qur'an, and He exhorts us to use intellect to understand it. How could it be possible, then, that it is

[161]Statement by Sufyan ibn 'Uyaynah when asked about the verses about the attributes

required of us to leave it without understanding it and knowing it by using the intellect". Until he says: "According to their understanding, the Prophets and the Messengers do not know the meanings of what Allah(سبحانه وتعالى) sends down to them from texts, neither do the angels nor the first and foremost of the generations of Islam. This means that either the meaning of what Allah(سبحانه وتعالى)describes Himself in the Qur'an, or most of it, is unknown to the Prophets, or that they pronounce words they do not understand their meaning." He says: "It is well known that this would be considered as defamation of the Qur'an and the Prophets. Allah(سبحانه وتعالى)sends down the Qur'an and informs us that He made it a guidance and an enlightenment for humankind, and commands the Prophet to convey it clearly and to explain to the people what has been sent down to them, and also enjoins contemplating the Qur'an and understanding it. Then, [could it be that the meaning of] the most honorable of knowledge; which is what Allah(سبحانه وتعالى) informs us about Himself of attributes or that He is the Creator of everything, or that He is the All-Knower, or that He has commanded and prohibited, promised and threatened, or what He has informed about the Hereafter, is unknown, so it cannot be understood or contemplated?! Therefore, the Prophet would not have explained to the people what has been sent down to them and neither would he have conveyed the message clearly?! If this is the case, then any atheist and innovator can say: 'The truth is what I have realized with my opinion and intellect. There is nothing in the text that contradicts this since these texts are problematic and unclear, and nobody knows its meaning. Therefore, it is not plausible to use something unknown as evidence.'

These words would effectively close the door of guidance and enlightenment on the Prophets' part. However, it would open the door for those who oppose them, saying: Indeed, true guidance and enlightenment is in our methodology, not the methodology of the prophets; because we know what we are saying and can explain it with intellectual evidence, while the prophets do not even know what they are saying: so how can they explain its purpose? It is thus clear that the statement of the people of Tafweed [pass over the meanings], who claim that they are the followers of Sunnah and the Salaf, is amongst the most dangerous of statements of the people of innovations and atheism."

It is the End of the Saying of Ibn Taimiyah (رحمه الله).

The Interpretation [التأويل]

Linguistic Meaning of interpretation: Returning the thing to its intended purpose [origin]; it comes from the word al-awl[The First], which means returning.

Conventional Meaning: Returning the word to its intended purpose by explaining its meaning or implication. It is used to refer to three meanings:

The first meaning: "Tafseer"[exegesis]; to explain the words by stating the intended meaning. As Allah(سبحانه وتعالى) mentions about the two companions of prison addressing Yusuf:

[162]﴿...نَبِّئْنَا بِتَأْوِيلِهِ...﴾

"Inform us of its interpretation."Also, the saying of the Prophet ﷺ for Ibn 'Abbâs رضي الله عنه, also indicates this meaning: "O Allah make him acquire a deep understanding of the religion and teach him the interpretation of things"[163]. Likewise, the saying of Ibn 'Abbâs رضي الله عنه, which we have

[162] Yusuf: 36
[163] Ahmad, (1/266,314); Hakim, (3/534) and he says it is authentic; Ibn Hibban in his Sahih (7015); al-Bukhari, Book of Washing, Chapter: Putting water when

mentioned previously: "I am one of those who are firmly grounded in knowledge and know the deep interpretation of it". Additionally, Ibn Jarir and other exegetists say: "تأويل قوله تعالى" means its interpretation [its commentary]. The meaning of Ta'weel (interpretation) is known to the scholars.

The second meaning: To return the word to its reality. If it is information, then its interpretation will be the reality of the informed thing. This interpretation is used for Allah(سبحانه وتعالى)'s Being, and His Essence and Attributes, which no one knows it's true reality except Allah(سبحانه وتعالى). If it is a request, then its interpretation will be fulfilling the requested thing.

Example of an Information: Allah(سبحانه وتعالى) says:

﴿هَلْ يَنظُرُونَ إِلاَّ تَأْوِيلَهُ...﴾[164]

"Await they just for the final fulfillment of the event?"

It means that they are only waiting for the actualization of what they have been informed about from resurrection and recompense. Allah(سبحانه وتعالى) says about Yusuf ﷺ:

﴿...هَذَا تَأْوِيلُ رُؤْيَايَ مِن قَبْلُ قَدْ جَعَلَهَا رَبِّي حَقًّا...﴾[165]

"This is the interpretation of my dream aforetime! My Lord has made it come true!"

Example of A Request: 'Aisha ﷺ says: in Ruku' and Sujud Prophet ﷺ used to repeat more and more of "سبحانك اللهم ربنا و بحمدك اللهم اغفرلي"[How perfect You are O Allah(سبحانه وتعالى), our Lord and I

---

releasing (143); Muslim, Book of virtue of the companions (2477) the first part only.

[164] Al-A'raf: 53

[165] Yoosuf: 100

praise You. O Allah(سبحانه وتعالى) forgive me]. By saying this, he was doing Ta'weel [interpretation] of Qur'an; this means he was fulfilling the command of

Allah(سبحانه وتعالى), when He says:

﴿إِذَا جَاءَ نَصْرُ اللَّهِ وَالْفَتْحُ * وَرَأَيْتَ النَّاسَ يَدْخُلُونَ فِي دِينِ اللَّهِ أَفْوَاجًا * فَسَبِّحْ بِحَمْدِ رَبِّكَ وَاسْتَغْفِرْهُ إِنَّهُ كَانَ تَوَّابًا﴾[166]

"When comes the Help of Allah (to you, O Muhammad against your enemies) and the conquest (of Makkah), * And you see that the people enter Allah's religion (Islam) in crowds *So glorify the Praises of your Lord, and ask for His Forgiveness. Verily, He is the One Who accepts the repentance and forgives."

Additionally, you may say, "So and so does not deal with usury since he is fulfilling the interpretation of the verse:

﴿...وَأَحَلَّ اللَّهُ الْبَيْعَ وَحَرَّمَ الرِّبَا...﴾[167]

"Whereas Allah has permitted trading and forbidden Riba(usury)."

However, this kind of Ta'weel does not exist unless it takes place, only then can it be fulfilled.

As for Allah(سبحانه وتعالى)'s saying:

﴿...وَمَا يَعْلَمُ تَأْوِيلَهُ إِلاَّ اللَّهُ وَالرَّاسِخُونَ فِي الْعِلْمِ يَقُولُونَ آمَنَّا بِهِ كُلٌّ مِّنْ عِندِ رَبِّنَا...﴾[168]

"But none knows its hidden meanings save Allah. And those who are firmly grounded in knowledge say: 'We believe in it; the whole of it (clear and unclear Verses) are from our Lord.'"

---

[166] An-Nasr: 1-3
[167] Al-Baqarah: 275
[168] Ali 'Imran: 7

Based on the stop or continuity [tajweed techniques], there are two possible interpretations; either the intended meaning is simply the meaning or returning the words to their reality. When we stop at﴿إِلَّا ٱللَّهُ﴾, the Ta'weel will be according to the second meaning, which is "returning the word to its reality". This is because no one knows the reality of what Allah(سبحانه وتعالى) has informed us about Himself and about the Hereafter except Allah(سبحانه وتعالى) Himself. However, if we continue the recitation, then the Ta'weel will be according to the first meaning which is Tafseer because those who are firmly grounded in knowledge know its interpretations well, and it is not specific to Allah(سبحانه وتعالى).

Therefore, we know that the meaning of Istiwâ is Highness and Stability; this is the known Ta'weel to us. However, we do not know its true matter of being and reality; this is the unknown Ta'weel to us. Likewise, we know the meaning of what Allah(سبحانه وتعالى)has informed us about His Names and Attributes, and we can differentiate among these meanings. We know the meaning of life, knowledge, power, hearing, seeing and so on. We also know that life is not knowledge, knowledge is not power, power is not hearing, hearing is not the seeing, and so on for the rest of the Names and Attributes. However, we do not know the reality and essence of these meanings when used in reference to Allah(سبحانه وتعالى).

These two meanings of Ta'weel are known in the Qur'an, Sunnah and in the statement of the Salaf.

The third meaning of Ta'weel: To exchange the probable meaning of the text to the less probable meaning, as entailed by evidence. Alternatively, you may say, exchanging the literal meaning of the text to a meaning that opposes the literal meaning, as entailed by evidence. This is the conventional definition for many of the late scholars, who spoke in matters of Fiqh and its Usul. Additionally, this [definition] is what most of the contemporaries, who have spoken about the interpretation of the texts of the attributes, are concerned about, and whether [its usage] is praiseworthy or blameworthy? Or whether it is right or wrong?

Inquiry: If this [alternative] meaning is proven by authentic evidence, then applying it is correct and praiseworthy and would be considered the first definition of Ta'weel, which is Tafseer [exegesis].

This is because the exegesis of a text is interpreting it as per the intent of the speaker, whether it is according to its apparent meaning or the opposite of its apparent meaning, so long as we know the intent of the speaker.

Example of this: Allah(سبحانه وتعالى) says:

﴿أَتَى أَمْرُ اللَّهِ فَلاَ تَسْتَعْجِلُوهُ...﴾[169]

"The Event (the Hour or the punishment of disbelievers and polytheists or the Islamic laws or commandments), ordained by Allah will come to pass, so seek not to hasten it."

Allah(سبحانه وتعالى)is warning His slaves about something that will happen in the future, not about something that has already happened and passed, as is entailed by His saying:﴿فَلاَ تَسْتَعْجِلُوهُ﴾. [Yet, according to the literal meaning of the first part, it seems that it has already happened.] Likewise,

Allah(سبحانه وتعالى) says:

﴿فَإِذَا قَرَأْتَ الْقُرْآنَ فَاسْتَعِذْ بِاللَّهِ مِنَ الشَّيْطَانِ الرَّجِيمِ﴾[170]

"So when you want to recite the Qur'an, seek refuge with Allah from Shaitan (Satan), the outcast (the cursed one)."

[169] An-Nahl: 1
[170] Ibid: 98

From the literal meaning of the text, it seems that the command is for when you have finished the recitation of the Qur'an [which is usually entailed by using the past tense قرأت]. However, the intent here is 'if you want to recite'. This is because the Prophet ﷺ used to seek refuge before recitation, not after the recitation.

However, if [the alternative meaning] is not proven by authentic evidence, then it is wrong and blameworthy, and it should be called misinterpretation, not interpretation.

Example of this, Allah(سبحانه وتعالى) says:

﴿الرَّحْمَنُ عَلَى الْعَرْشِ اسْتَوَى﴾[171]

"The Most Beneficent (Allah) Istawa(rose over) the (Mighty) Throne (in a manner that suits His Majesty)."

The literal meaning of this verse is that Allah(سبحانه وتعالى)has been raised over the Throne, in a manner that is befitting His majesty; and this is the intended meaning. Therefore, reinterpreting it to mean that He has conquered and owned [the Throne] is a wrong and blameworthy interpretation, and is considered an alteration of the statement from its place; because there is no authentic evidence for it.

Muhkam(Clarity/ Unambiguity) and Mutashâbih (Ambiguity)

Allah(سبحانه وتعالى) describes the Qur'an as Muhkam [Certainty/Clarity], Mutashâbih [entirely not clear/Ambiguity], or that some of its parts are Muhkam while some others are Mutashâbih.

As for the first description, Allah(سبحانه وتعالى) says:

---

[171]Taha: 5

﴿الر تِلْكَ آيَاتُ الْكِتَابِ الْحَكِيمِ﴾[172]

"Alif-Lâm-Ra. [These letters are one of the miracles of the Qur'an, and none but Allah(alone) knows their meanings]. These are the Verses of the Book (the Qur'an) Al-Hakim [showing lawful and unlawful things, explaining Allah's (Divine) Laws for mankind, leading them to eternal happiness by ordering them to follow the true Islamic Monotheism, - worshipping none but Allah Alone - that will guide them to Paradise and save them from Hell]."

As for the second description, Allah(سبحانه وتعالى) says:

﴿اللَّهُ نَزَّلَ أَحْسَنَ الْحَدِيثِ كِتَابًا مُّتَشَابِهًا...﴾[173]

"Allah has sent down the best statement, a Book (this Qur'an), its parts resembling each other in goodness and truth."

As for the third description, Allah(سبحانه وتعالى) says:

﴿هُوَ الَّذِي أَنزَلَ عَلَيْكَ الْكِتَابَ مِنْهُ آيَاتٌ مُّحْكَمَاتٌ هُنَّ أُمُّ الْكِتَابِ وَأُخَرُ مُتَشَابِهَاتٌ...﴾[174]

"It is He Who has sent down to you (Muhammad) the Book (this Qur'an). In it are Verses that are entirely clear, they are the foundations of the Book [and those are the Verses of Al-Ahkam(commandments, etc.), Al-Fara'id(obligatory duties) and Al-Hudud(legal laws for the punishment of thieves, adulterers, etc.)]; and others not entirely clear."

When referring to the whole Qur'an as Muhkam, it means the excellence and quality of its words and meanings. Indeed, all the words of the Qur'an are perfectly expressive, eloquent and coherent. Its meanings are the most perfect of meanings, the noblest and most beneficial for the

[172]Yoonus: 1
[173]Az-Zumar: 23
[174]Ali 'Imran: 7

creation since they contain complete authentic information and perfect guidance and justice in all commandments.

As Allah(سبحانه وتعالى)says:

﴿وَتَمَّتْ كَلِمَتُ رَبِّكَ صِدْقًا وَعَدْلاً...﴾[175]

"And the Word of your Lord has been fulfilled in truth and injustice."

When referring to the whole Qur'an as Mutashaabih, it means the Qur'an's consistency in perfection, accuracy, and coherence. Indeed, it does not contradict each other in matters of legislation and none of it falsifies other parts in matters of information. Allah(سبحانه وتعالى)says:

﴿أَفَلاَ يَتَدَبَّرُونَ الْقُرْآنَ وَلَوْ كَانَ مِنْ عِندِ غَيْرِ اللّهِ لَوَجَدُواْ فِيهِ اخْتِلاَفًا كَثِيرًا﴾[176]

"Do they not then consider the Qur'an carefully? Had it been from other than Allah, they would surely have found therein many contradictions."

When referring to some of the Qur'an as Muhkam, it means its clarity and manifestation; its meaning is clear and obvious, not ambiguous. This is usually the case for many of the information and legislation.

Example for the information: Allah(سبحانه وتعالى) says:

﴿شَهْرُ رَمَضَانَ الَّذِيَ أُنزِلَ فِيهِ الْقُرْآنُ...﴾[177]

"The month of Ramadan in which was revealed the Qur'an."

Everybody knows the month of Ramadan as well as the Qur'an.

Example for the legislation: Allah(سبحانه وتعالى) says:

---

[175] Al-An'am: 115
[176] An-Nisa': 82
[177] Al-Baqarah: 185

﴿...وَبِالْوَالِدَيْنِ إِحْسَانًا...﴾[178]

"And do good to parents."

Everybody knows who his or her parents are and what good behavior is.

And when referring to some of the Qur'an as Mutashâbih, it means its ambiguity whereupon the meaning is hidden so that it may be ambiguous to some people, but not to everyone; indeed, only the firmly grounded people in knowledge know it, not others.

Our Stance regarding these Divergent Descriptions and How to reconcile between them

Our stance on these different descriptions and how to combine them is as follows: it is not contradictory to describe the whole Qur'an as both entirely Muhkam and entirely Mutashaabih. We can combine between them by saying: the excellent and accurate speech resembles each other in perfection and truthfulness. There are no any contradictions in its legislation and its information does not falsify its other reports.

Moreover, it is not contradictory to describe some parts of the Qur'an as Muhkam, while some others as Mutashaabih. This is because each of these descriptions is in its specific place; both of them do not coincide in the same part. Some parts of the Qur'an are Muhkam, which means that they are entirely clear; while some others are Mutashaabih, so their meaning is hidden and not clear.

People are divided into two groups in this issue:

[178] An-Nisa': 36

People firmly grounded in knowledge say: We believe in it; the whole of it [clear and unclear verses] is from our Lord. And if it comes from Him, then there shall not be any ambiguity therein that will decree misguidance or contradiction. They try to understand the Mutashaabih through Muhkam, so they use the Muhkam as interpretation for the Mutashaabih verses.

As for people of misguidance, they chase after the ambiguous verses, and make it a subject of doubt and instilling doubt; therefore, they become misguided and misguide other people. Moreover, they assume, through these ambiguous verses, things that are not befitting of Allah(سبحانه وتعالى), His Book or His Messenger ﷺ.

The first example[179]: Allah(سبحانه وتعالى)says:

﴿إِنَّا نَحْنُ نُحْيِي الْمَوْتَى...﴾[180]

"Verily, We give life to the dead."

And Allah(سبحانه وتعالى) says:

﴿إِنَّا نَحْنُ نَزَّلْنَا الذِّكْرَ وَإِنَّا لَهُ لَحَافِظُونَ﴾[181]

"Verily We: It is We Who have sent down the Dhikr (i.e. the Qur'an) and surely, We will guard it (from corruption)."

And other verses like these, where Allah(سبحانه وتعالى)uses the plural pronoun to refer to Himself [We]. The Christian follows this type of ambiguity [Mutashaabih] and based on this, they claim a plurality of Allah(سبحانه وتعالى).In addition, they say Allah(سبحانه وتعالى) is the third of the three [Trinity]. However, they leave the Muhkam verse which clearly mentions that Allah(سبحانه وتعالى) is Only One.

[179] An assumption unbefitting of Allah
[180] Yasin: 12
[181] Al-Hijr: 9

As for those who are firmly grounded in knowledge: They deduce that plurality is indicative of His Greatness, due to Allah(سبحانه وتعالى)'s many Noble Attributes. They understand this Mutashaabih verse through another Muhkam verse, where Allah(سبحانه وتعالى)says:

﴿وَإِلَٰهُكُمْ إِلَٰهٌ وَاحِدٌ لاَّ إِلَٰهَ إِلاَّ هُوَ...﴾[182]

"And your Ilah(God) is One Ilah(God - Allah), La ilahaillaHuwa(there is none who has the right to be worshipped but He)."

They say to the Christian man: The claim that you have conjured – due to your confusion – is the reason for Allah(سبحانه وتعالى) to consider you a disbeliever and a liar. Listen to the Allah(سبحانه وتعالى) saying:

﴿لَّقَدْ كَفَرَ الَّذِينَ قَالُواْ إِنَّ اللَّهَ ثَالِثُ ثَلاثَةٍ وَمَا مِنْ إِلَٰهٍ إِلاَّ إِلَٰهٌ وَاحِدٌ...﴾[183]

"Surely, disbelievers are those who said: 'Allah is the third of the three (in a Trinity).' But there is no ilah(god) (none who has the right to be worshipped) but One Ilah (God - Allah(سبحانه وتعالى))."

Means they have disbelieved by saying "Allah(سبحانه وتعالى) is the third of the three".

The second example[184]: Allah(سبحانه وتعالى) says about His Prophet ﷺ:

﴿إِنَّكَ لا تَهْدِي مَنْ أَحْبَبْتَ...﴾[185]

"Verily! You (O Muhammad) guide not whom you like."

And Allah(سبحانه وتعالى) says:

﴿...وَإِنَّكَ لَتَهْدِي إِلَى صِرَاطٍ مُّسْتَقِيمٍ﴾[186]

---

[182]Baqarah: 163
[183] Al-Ma'idah: 73
[184] Assumption about the Qur'an that is not appropriated with it.
[185] Al-Qasas: 56

"And verily, you (O Muhammad) are indeed guiding (mankind) to the Straight Path (i.e. Allah's religion of Islamic Monotheism)."

Those whose hearts have deviated from the right path assume that these two verses contradict each other; the contradiction is that the negation in the first verse and an affirmation in the second verse. Therefore, they say there is a contradiction in the Qur'an.

As for those who are firmly grounded in knowledge, they say: there is no contradiction between these two verses. In the first verse, the intended guidance is the guidance of Tawfeeq [success]; success only belongs to Allah(سبحانه وتعالى), neither does the Messenger ﷺ have any authority over it nor do others. In the second verse, the intended guidance is the guidance of direction; [direction to the true path] can be from Allah(سبحانه وتعالى)as well as from others – the messengers and their inheritors from the scholars.

The third example[187]: Allah(سبحانه وتعالى) says about His Prophet ﷺ,

﴿فَإِن كُنتَ فِي شَكٍّ مِّمَّا أَنزَلْنَا إِلَيْكَ فَاسْأَلِ الَّذِينَ يَقْرَؤُونَ الْكِتَابَ مِن قَبْلِكَ لَقَدْ جَاءَكَ الْحَقُّ مِن رَّبِّكَ فَلاَ تَكُونَنَّ مِنَ الْمُمْتَرِينَ﴾[188]

"So if you (O Muhammad) are in doubt concerning that which We have revealed unto you, [i.e. that your name is written in the Taurat (Torah) and the Injeel (Gospel)] then ask those who are reading the Book [the Taurat (Torah) and the Injeel (Gospel)] before you. Verily, the truth has come to you from your Lord. So be not of those who doubt (it)."

Those whose hearts have deviated from the right path assume that the Prophet ﷺhas doubts about what has been revealed to him. Therefore, they slander the Prophet ﷺ.

---

[186] Ash-Shura: 52

[187] An example of an inappropriate assumption about the Messenger ﷺ.

[188] Yoonus: 94

As for those who are firmly grounded in knowledge, they say: Prophet ﷺ has no doubt or confusion about what has been revealed to him. How could it be possible when Allah(سبحانه وتعالى)bears witness about his faith by saying:

﴿آمَنَ الرَّسُولُ بِمَا أُنزِلَ إِلَيْهِ مِن رَّبِّهِ وَالْمُؤْمِنُونَ كُلٌّ آمَنَ بِاللَّهِ وَمَلائِكَتِهِ وَكُتُبِهِ وَرُسُلِهِ لاَ نُفَرِّقُ بَيْنَ أَحَدٍ مِّن رُّسُلِهِ...﴾[189]

"The Messenger (Muhammad) believes in what has been sent down to him from his Lord, and (so do) the believers. Each one believes in Allah, His Angels, His Books, and His Messengers."

Allah(سبحانه وتعالى) says:

﴿...فَآمِنُواْ بِاللَّهِ وَرَسُولِهِ النَّبِيِّ الأُمِّيِّ الَّذِي يُؤْمِنُ بِاللَّهِ وَكَلِمَاتِهِ وَاتَّبِعُوهُ لَعَلَّكُمْ تَهْتَدُونَ﴾[190]

"So believe in Allah and His Messenger (Muhammad), the Prophet who can neither read nor write (i.e. Muhammad) who believes in Allah and His Words [(this Qur'an), the Taurat (Torah) and the Injeel (Gospel) and also Allah's Word: "Be!" - and he was, i.e. 'Esa (Jesus) son of Maryam (Mary),], and follow him so that you may be guided."

They say: This [conditional] expression - ﴿فَإِن كُنتَ فِي شَكٍّ﴾ - does not necessitate for the condition to be fulfilled; in fact, it is not possible for it to be fulfilled. As Allah(سبحانه وتعالى) says:

﴿قُلْ إِن كَانَ لِلرَّحْمَنِ وَلَدٌ فَأَنَا أَوَّلُ الْعَابِدِينَ﴾[191]

"Say (O Muhammad): "If the Most Beneficent

(Allah(سبحانه وتعالى)) had a son (or children as you pretend), then I am the first of Allah's worshippers."

[189] Al-Baqarah: 285
[190] Al-A'raf: 158
[191] Az-Zukhruf: 81

Indeed, it is absolutely impossible for Allah(سبحانه وتعالى)to have a son, as Allah(سبحانه وتعالى) says:

﴿وَمَا يَنبَغِي لِلرَّحْمَنِ أَن يَتَّخِذَ وَلَدًا﴾[192]

"But it is not suitable for (the Majesty of) the Most Beneficent (Allah) that He should beget a son (or offspring or children)."

Likewise, for the Messenger ﷺ to be doubtful or confused about what has been revealed to him is absolutely impossible. However, the expression comes in the form of a conditional statement to emphasize the impossibility of doubt and confusion coming from the Messenger ﷺ about what has been revealed to him.

If you ask: What is the wisdom for some of the Qur'an to be Mutashaabih?

Answer: The wisdom behind this is to test the slaves to ascertain who the true believer is and who is doubtful, ignorant and misguided. The true believer who has deep knowledge believes in Allah(سبحانه وتعالى) and His words and knows that the speech of Allah(سبحانه وتعالى) contains no contradiction or discrepancies. Therefore, he interprets the Mutashaabih through Muhkam; in essence, all of it becomes Muhkam. As for those in whose hearts there is a deviation, they follow the Mutashâbih verses in order to misinterpret the Book of Allah(سبحانه وتعالى)using its very verses. They are misguided and they misguide others; they become the leaders of misguidance and wretchedness. They tempt people away from their religion by instilling doubt and confusion. In turn, they misguide each other.

Allah(سبحانه وتعالى) says:

[192] Maryam: 92

﴿...فَأَمَّا الَّذِينَ فِي قُلُوبِهِمْ زَيْغٌ فَيَتَّبِعُونَ مَا تَشَابَهَ مِنْهُ ابْتِغَاء الْفِتْنَةِ وَابْتِغَاء تَأْوِيلِهِ وَمَا يَعْلَمُ تَأْوِيلَهُ إِلاَّ اللّهُ وَالرَّاسِخُونَ فِي الْعِلْمِ يَقُولُونَ آمَنَّا بِهِ كُلٌّ مِّنْ عِندِ رَبِّنَا وَمَا يَذَّكَّرُ إِلاَّ أُوْلُواْ الأَلْبَابِ * رَبَّنَا لاَ تُزِغْ قُلُوبَنَا بَعْدَ إِذْ هَدَيْتَنَا وَهَبْ لَنَا مِن لَّدُنكَ رَحْمَةً إِنَّكَ أَنتَ الْوَهَّابُ﴾[193]

"So as for those in whose hearts there is a deviation (from the truth) they follow that which is not entirely clear thereof, seeking Al-Fitnah (polytheism and trials, etc.), and seeking for its hidden meanings, but none knows its hidden meanings save Allah. And those who are firmly grounded in knowledge say: "We believe in it; the whole of it (clear and unclear Verses) are from our Lord." And none receive admonition except men of understanding. (Tafsir At-Tabari). * (They say): "Our Lord! Let not our hearts deviate (from the truth) after You have guided us, and grant us mercy from You. Truly, You are the Bestower."

Conclusion

Two Types of Tashâbuh [entirely not clear] in the Qur'an are Actual and Relative

Actual: Nobody knows it except Allah(سبحانه وتعالى), such as, the reality about what Allah(سبحانه وتعالى) has informed about Himself and about Hereafter. We – although we know the meaning of this information –yet, we do not know the essence and the reality of it, as Allah(سبحانه وتعالى) says:

﴿يَعْلَمُ مَا بَيْنَ أَيْدِيهِمْ وَمَا خَلْفَهُمْ وَلا يُحِيطُونَ بِهِ عِلْمًا﴾[194]

"He (Allah(سبحانه وتعالى)) knows what happens to them (His creatures) in this world, and what will happen to them (in the Hereafter), and they will never compass anything of His Knowledge."

---

[193] Ali 'Imran: 7-8
[194] Taha: 110

He also says:

﴿لاَّ تُدْرِكُهُ الأَبْصَارُ وَهُوَ يُدْرِكُ الأَبْصَارَ...﴾[195]

"No vision can grasp Him, but His Grasp is over all vision."

He says about what have in Hereafter:

﴿فَلا تَعْلَمُ نَفْسٌ مَّا أُخْفِيَ لَهُم مِّن قُرَّةِ أَعْيُنٍ جَزَاء بِمَا كَانُوا يَعْمَلُونَ...﴾[196]

"No person knows what is kept hidden for them of joy as a reward for what they used to do."

In the authentic Hadith Qudsi[197], reported in the Saheehayn [Bukhari and Muslim], the Prophet ﷺ narrates that Allah(سبحانه وتعالى)says: "I have prepared for my righteous slaves what no eye has seen, no ear has heard, and the mind of no man has conceived".[198]

Some of the terms used in the information Allah(سبحانه وتعالى) gives about Himself and the hereafter resemble things we know in this world. For example, He says about Himself that He is Alive, Knowledgeable, Powerful, Hearer and Seer and so on. We know that these attributes are not actually the same as their counterparts when they are used to describe the creation. Indeed, its true reality is not known except to Allah(سبحانه وتعالى). Moreover, we know that in Heaven there is meat, milk, honey, water and wine and so on. However, their essence is not the same as their counterparts in this world; therefore, no one knows its reality except Allah(سبحانه وتعالى).

Any information about the unseen world will not be understood unless they are expressed in known terms, whose meanings are known in the

---

[195] Al-An'am: 103
[196] As-Sajdah: 17
[197] Hadith Qudsi
[198] Al-Bukhari, Chapter: Beginning of the Creation, Chapter: Attributes of the Heavens, no. 3244.

observable world. Thus, the unseen things can be understood through knowledge about these observed things; while realizing the big difference and that the foretold unseen is more magnificent than the known observable. Therefore, no one should inquire about this type [of information], which is not known except to Allah(سبحانه وتعالى), because of the inability to grasp it.

Relative: It is unclear to some people while clear to others. Those who are firmly grounded in knowledge and faith know about it, while others do not know. It is either due to their deficient knowledge, or due to their negligence in inquiring about it, or deficient understanding or their bad intention.

This type [of information] should be inquired about because it is possible to attain it. Indeed, there is nothing in the Qur'an that is unknown to everyone [i.e. someone must know about it]. Allah(سبحانه وتعالى) says:

﴿...وَنَزَّلْنَا عَلَيْكَ الْكِتَابَ تِبْيَانًا لِّكُلِّ شَيْءٍ...﴾[199]

"And We have sent down to you the Book (the Qur'an) as an exposition of everything."

And He says:

﴿هَذَا بَيَانٌ لِّلنَّاسِ وَهُدًى وَمَوْعِظَةٌ لِّلْمُتَّقِينَ﴾[200]

"This (the Qur'an) is a plain statement for mankind, a guidance and instruction to those who are Al-Muttaqun."

And He says:

﴿فَإِذَا قَرَأْنَاهُ فَاتَّبِعْ قُرْآنَهُ * ثُمَّ إِنَّ عَلَيْنَا بَيَانَهُ﴾[201]

---

[199] An-Nahl: 89
[200] Ali 'Imran: 138

"It is for Us to collect it and to give you (O Muhammad) the ability to recite it (the Qur'an) * And when We have recited it to you [O Muhammad through Jibrael (Gabriel)], then follow you its (the Qur'an's) recital."

And He says:

﴿يَا أَيُّهَا النَّاسُ قَدْ جَاءَكُم بُرْهَانٌ مِّن رَّبِّكُمْ وَأَنزَلْنَا إِلَيْكُمْ نُورًا مُّبِينًا﴾[202]

"O mankind! Verily, there has come to you a convincing proof (Prophet Muhammad) from your Lord, and We sent down to you a manifest light (this Qur'an)."

And He says:

﴿شَهْرُ رَمَضَانَ الَّذِي أُنزِلَ فِيهِ الْقُرْآنُ هُدًى لِّلنَّاسِ وَبَيِّنَاتٍ مِّنَ الْهُدَى وَالْفُرْقَانِ...﴾[203]

"The month of Ramadan in which was revealed the Qur'an, a guidance for mankind and clear proofs for the guidance and the criterion (between right and wrong)."

There are many examples of this type in the informational, knowledge-based issues, as well as the legislative, action-based issues. Most of the disagreed upon issues, or all of it belongs to this type.

Informational, Knowledge-Based Example

Allah(سبحانه وتعالى)says:

﴿...لَيْسَ كَمِثْلِهِ شَيْءٌ...﴾[204]

"There is nothing like unto Him."

---

[201] Al-Qiyamah: 17-18
[202] An-Nisa': 174
[203] Al-Baqarah: 185
[204] Ash-Shura: 11

This statement confuses the people who suspend the meaning of the verse; they understand from it the non-existence of Allah(سبحانه وتعالى)'s Attributes. They assume that affirming the Attributes necessitates likening Allah (سبحانه وتعالى)to His creation. Therefore, they negate all that Allah(سبحانه وتعالى)has informed about Himself or some of it. They deny the textual evidence as well as the intellectual evidence that affirm Allah(سبحانه وتعالى)'s Attributes of perfection. They have overlooked the fact that sharing similar meanings does not necessitate resemblance in reality.

If they carefully examine this negated statement,

﴿لَيْسَ كَمِثْلِهِ شَيْءٌ﴾ "There is nothing like unto Him, "it would have been clear to them that it implies the affirmation of the attributes, not their negation. Indeed, negating resemblance indicates the affirmation of the original meaning. However, because of Allah(سبحانه وتعالى)'s perfection, nothing resembles Him; neither in His Being nor in His Attributes. If the original attribute was not affirmed, then negating any similarity would not have been beneficial.

Legislative, Action-Based Example: Prophet ﷺ says: "Pray as you saw me praying."[205] This statement confuses some people so they think it pertains to both the quantity [how many Rak'ât he prayed] and the quality [how he prayed]. Thus, they think it is not allowed to pray more than what Prophet ﷺ used to pray at night; so, it would not be allowed to pray in Ramadan more than eleven or thirteen Rak'ât. On the other hand, whoever ponders upon the Hadith, he will realize that it pertains to the quality only, and not the quantity; unless the quantity is inclusive of the quality, such as the number of Rak'âts in one prayer. This is proven by the Hadith that is reported in al-Bukhari and in other books, which is narrated by Abdullah Ibn 'Umar رضي الله عنهما: "Someone asked the

[205] Al-Bukhari: Book of Adhân, Chapter: Adhân for travelers if they are in a group No. 631.

Prophet ﷺ when he was on the Minbar, 'What is your opinion about the night prayer?' Prophet said, 'Two, two; yet, when you fear the approach of the morning, then pray one Rak'at, so that it will be considered as Witr for what you have prayed.'" In another narration, the questioner asks, "How is night prayer [done]?" If the number of the Rak'ât is restricted, then the Prophet would have explained it to the questioner. Hence, the preferred opinion is that it is better to limit the night prayer to eleven or thirteen Rak'ât; however, if someone prays more than there is no harm.

There are many examples regarding this issue that is available in the books of Fiqh, which examine differences of opinion and the preferred statements. Indeed, it is

Allah(سبحانه وتعالى) (Alone) Whose help can be sought.

The Sixth Principle

Guidelines for Affirming and Negating What is Possible and Impossible for Allah(سبحانه وتعالى)

The Attributes of Allah(سبحانه وتعالى) the Highest revolve around negation and affirmation – as is mentioned previously – therefore, there need to be guidelines for both.

Guidelines for Negation, the following are negated on behalf of

Allah(سبحانه وتعالى) the Most High:

First: All imperfect attributes, such as blindness, deafness, muteness, sleep, death and so on.

Second: Any deficiency in His perfection, like a deficiency in His Life, Knowledge, Power, Honor, Wisdom and so on.

Third: Resemblance to the creation, such as likening His knowledge with the knowledge of the creation, or His face with the face of the creation, or His rising over the Throne with the rising of His creation and so on.

Evidence for the First Criterion of Negation:

Allah(سبحانه وتعالى) says:

﴿...وَلِلَّهِ الْمَثَلُ الأَعْلَىَ...﴾[206]

"And for Allah(سبحانه وتعالى) is the highest description."

In this example, affirming the highest description, which is the noblest of attributes, necessitates the negation of all imperfections.

Evidence for the Second Criterion of Negation: Allah(سبحانه وتعالى) says:

﴿وَلَقَدْ خَلَقْنَا السَّمَاوَاتِ وَالأَرْضَ وَمَا بَيْنَهُمَا فِي سِتَّةِ أَيَّامٍ وَمَا مَسَّنَا مِن لُّغُوبٍ﴾[207]

"And indeed We created the heavens and the earth and all between them in six Days and nothing of fatigue touched Us."

Evidence for the Third Criterion of Negation: Allah(سبحانه وتعالى) says:

﴿...لَيْسَ كَمِثْلِهِ شَيْءٌ...﴾[208]

"There is nothing like unto Him."

---

[206] An-Nahl: 60
[207] Qaf: 38
[208] Ash-Shura: 11

Therefore, the guidelines for negation cannot be solely based on negating resemblance. This is due to two reasons:

Firstly:

If the purpose of negation is negating resemblance absolutely [التشابة المطلق] – i.e. negating equivalence in all aspects between the Creator and the creation, – then, this is a futile effort. Indeed, no one has ever claimed that the Creator is equivalent to the creation in every aspect; whereupon all that is affirmed for one – the possible, impossible and necessary – will also be affirmed for the other. It is impossible for any sane person, who realizes [the consequences of] such a claim, to say such a statement; since such negation is necessarily known by way of reason and common sense. Therefore, if that is the case, then such a negation has no benefit.

On the other hand, if the purpose of negation is negating general resemblance [مطلق التشابة] – i.e. negating similarities in some aspects, – then, this negation is invalid. Indeed, there are no two things except that they share some common characteristics and are different from each other in some other specific characteristics. So they are similar in some aspects while different in some other.

Life, for example, this is a common characteristic between the Creator and the creation. Allah the Highest says:

﴿وَتَوَكَّلْ عَلَى الْحَيِّ الَّذِي لا يَمُوتُ...﴾[209]

"And put your trust (O Muhammad) in the Ever Living One Who dies not."

Allah(سبحانه وتعالى) says:

﴿يُخْرِجُ الْحَيَّ مِنَ الْمَيِّتِ وَيُخْرِجُ الْمَيِّتَ مِنَ الْحَيِّ...﴾[210]

---

[209] Al-Furqan: 58

"He brings out the living from the dead, and brings out the dead from the living."

However, the Life of the Creator is unique to Him. Indeed, it is a perfect life from all aspects, it is not preceded by non-existence, nor is it followed with extinction. It is contrary to the life of the creation, which is an imperfect life that is preceded by non-existence and followed with extinction.

And He(سبحانه وتعالى) says:

﴿كُلُّ مَنْ عَلَيْهَا فَانٍ * وَيَبْقَى وَجْهُ رَبِّكَ ذُو الْجَلَالِ وَالإِكْرَامِ﴾[211]

"Whatsoever is on it (the earth) will perish And the Face of your Lord full of Majesty and Honor will abide forever."

The common characteristic, the "general life," [مطلق الحياة] is general and it is not special to anyone of them. However, their unique and special characteristics are not shared. Thus, there is no harm to share in this general meaning; what is prohibited is to make one share in the others' unique characteristics.

Then, this purpose – meaning, negating general resemblance – necessitates absolute suspension. If the attribute of Existence is negated from Allah(سبحانه وتعالى), for example, on grounds that the creature also has the attribute of existence and so affirming it for *Allah*(سبحانه وتعالى)necessitates resemblance, according to this conjecture, then, this negation would necessarily imply that the Creator is non-existence. In addition to this false implication, it will further necessitate another type of resemblance; resembling the Creator with the non-existence since they share in the same characteristic of nonexistence. Thus, such a methodology will necessitate that He

[210] Al-Rum: 19
[211] Ar-Rahman: 26-27

resembles the non-existence. Moreover, once existence and non-existence are both negated, then this necessitates a third type of resemblance, which is the most severe; it is a resemblance to the impossible; since existence and non-existence are opposites, they can neither be both negated or both affirmed.

If someone says: If something shares with another thing in any aspect, then whatever is possible for one in that aspect will be possible for the other, whatever is impossible for one will be impossible for the other, and whatever is necessary for one will be necessary for the other!

The answer will be from two angles:

- Prevention, it will be said to them: sharing a general characteristic [اصل الصفة] between the Creator and the creation does not necessitate for them to equally share in what is possible, impossible or necessary for such a characteristic. Indeed, general sharing [مطلق المشاركة] does not necessitate equivalence.
- Acknowledgement, it will be said to them: Suppose that it is so, however, if this shared portion does not necessitate affirming what is impossible for Allah(سبحانه وتعالى), or negating what He is deserving of, then it is not an impossible [characterization]. Therefore, if they share in the attribute of existence, life, knowledge, power –while maintaining [their distinct qualities] and what is befitting and deserving for each one –, then this type of sharing is possible, there is no harm in it in general. In fact, affirming [this type of sharing] is of the basic necessities of existence. This is because any two existing beings must coexist in such a fashion. On the other hand, whoever negates this, then he must suspend the existence of all existing beings; because negating the shared portion necessitates general suspension [of all characteristics].

Whoever understands this issue properly will overcome most of these suspicious issues, and this will disclose for him the errors of many of the intellectuals in this regard.

The interpretation of Tashbeeh [Resemblance]

Secondly: The second reason that proves that the guidelines for negation cannot be solely based on negating resemblance:

The people differ in their interpretation of Tashbeeh [resemblance]; some interpret it in a way, which others do not consider to be Tashbeeh.

Example (From the Mu'tazilah and their followers): They consider whoever affirms for Allah(سبحانه وتعالى) Eternal Knowledge [علما قديما]or Eternal Power [قدرة قديمة] as people of Mushabbih or Mumaththil. Because according to the majority of their scholars Qidam"Eternity" is a unique characteristic of Allah(سبحانه وتعالى). So whoever affirms for Him Eternal Knowledge or Power, he affirms for Him the similitude.

The People of Affirmation Respond to them with Denial at times, and with Acknowledgement at times:

[Eternity of Knowledge and Power]

As for denial, they say: Eternity [القدم] is not unique for Allah(سبحانه وتعالى). The unique attribute of the Deity is what no one can be characterized by, such as being the Lord of the Worlds, that He is Powerful over all things, and that He is God, and so on. If you describe the Attributes with eternity as you describe the Being, then [such a description]does not necessitate being the god, or lord, and so on. This is just like the Prophet ﷺ being, for instance, described with having a beginning, as well as his characteristics having a beginning, yet this does not necessitate these are qualities of prophethood.

On this basis, affirming the eternity for His Attributes is not considered as Tashbeeh or Tamtheel.

As for acknowledgement, they say: Presuming that this meaning is considered Tashbeh and Tamthel according to some people's terminology; yet, it is not negated by the intellect or texts. Therefore, there is no harm in affirming it.

The Qur'an negates the termal-Mathal [Equivalent], al-Kuf'[Equal], and An-Nidd [Counterpart] and so on. Additionally, the term 'attribute' in the Arabic language - which is the language of the Qur'an – is not equivalent to the described object, nor is it equal to it, nor its counterpart; therefore, it is not among the things that are negated by the Qur'an.

It is obligatory to negate only what the textual and the intellectual evidence have negated.

Another example: Asha'riah and people who are like them, those people negate the Highness for Allah(سبحانه وتعالى) but they do not negate the life, knowledge, power and other attributes. They say: These attributes cannot exist without a body; however, the highness cannot exist without the body. Therefore, if we affirm this attribute, we must also affirm a body for Him. In addition, since bodies are similar, then this necessitates resemblance.

Those who affirm [Eternity of the Knowledge and Power], they respond to them sometimes by denying the first part, which is "the highness cannot exist without a body," sometimes by denying the second part, which is "the bodies are similar," sometimes by denying both of these parts, and sometimes by explanation. They say, if you mean by 'body' that which is formed of flesh, bone and other parts that are dependent on each other, or that need to external assistance, then that is impossible on behalf of Allah(سبحانه وتعالى), The Self-Subsistent [Free of all wants] and Worthy of all Praise. Additionally, affirming the attributes does not necessitate this for Him. However, if you mean by 'body' that which is self-sustained and situated, described with appropriate attributes for Him, then, this is an established truth for Allah(سبحانه وتعالى) and it does imply any imperfections.

Once the dispute about Tashbih among the people is clear, merely negating it becomes invalid. This is because it would necessitate the negation of Allah(سبحانه وتعالى)'s perfect attributes, according to those who claim that affirming these attributes would necessitate resemblance.

Therefore, the correct guideline for negation is what has been previously [mentioned] at the beginning of the chapter.

Anthropomorphism "الجسم", Space "التحيز"

Once it is clear that it is invalid for the guidelines for negation to be solely based on negating resemblance and that it is an incorrect path, then it is more incorrect for some people to base it on negating anthropomorphism [التجسيم]or occupying a region in space [تحيز].

When they refute those who describe Allah(سبحانه وتعالى) with deficiencies such as sadness, crying, illness, giving birth and so on, they say: if Allah(سبحانه وتعالى)is characterized with these, then [it would necessitate that] He is a body, who occupies space; yet, this is impossible. This is their refutation.

This is an invalid methodology; it does not fulfill the purpose, for several reasons:

- The word "الجسم" [body],"التحيز" [existing in space], "الجوهر"[substance] and other similar words are general and ambiguous; it cannot ascertain a truth or refute a falsehood. That is why they have never been mentioned in Allah(سبحانه وتعالى)'s description of Himself or His Names, neither in the affirmative nor in the negative. They have never been mentioned in the Qur'an or in the Sunnah, or even mentioned by the salaf and the Imâms of this Ummah. Rather, these are invented words that have been rejected by the salaf and the Imâms of this Ummah.
- Describing Allah(سبحانه وتعالى) with these deficiencies is clearly more invalid than describing Him with "التجسم"and"التحيز". It is well known that describing Allah(سبحانه وتعالى) with those deficiencies are considered as kufr[disbelief]; unlike [describing Him with] "التجسم"and"التحيز", since they are ambiguous and unclear.

If describing Allah(سبحانه وتعالى) with these deficiencies is clearly more invalid than describing Him with "الجسم"and"الحيز", then, it is not correct to use the ambiguous[terms] to prove the obvious [terms]. This is because evidence should be able to clarify the premise and is able to prove it; therefore, it must be clearer than the premise.

- Whoever describes Allah(سبحانه وتعالى) with these deficiencies can say that we are describing Him in this way; yet, we are not claiming the "التجسيم"and"التحيز", just as those who affirm the Attributes of perfection while negating the "التجسم"and"التحيز". Thus, both statements of those who describe Him with the Attributes of perfection and those who describe Him with the characteristics of deficiency will be the same. Therefore, responding to them will be in the same way, in that affirmation [of attributes of perfection] necessitates "التجسم"and"التحيز". That would indeed be absolutely invalid and erroneous.

- Those who base the guidelines for negation on negating "التجسم" and"التحيز", they have actually negated the Attributes of perfection. Describing Allah(سبحانه وتعالى) the Highest with the Attributes of perfection is a proven obligation, as is established by the texts and intellect. Thus, anything that would necessitate the negation [of this established obligation] is invalidated by the texts and intellect. In this way, the corruptness of this methodology and its invalidity is made clear.
- Those who adhere to this methodology contradict each other. Indeed, whoever affirms some [of the attributes] and negates others, the opponent may impose the implication of this affirmation; and whoever negates some [of the attributes] and affirms some others, the opponent may impose on him the implication of this negation.

Example of this: Those who affirm for Allah(سبحانه وتعالى)the attributes of Life, Knowledge, Power, Will, Hearing, Seeing and Speech, without the rest of the attributes, are accused by those who negate these, such as the Mu'tazilah, by saying: Affirming these attributes necessitates anthropomorphism; because these attributes are A'rad[212]and A'rad cannot be displayed without a body.

The other group responds to them by saying: You are affirming that

Allah(سبحانه وتعالى) is Alive, Knowledgeable and Powerful; yet, you are saying He has no body, although you do not know anything that is alive, knowledgeable and powerful except that it is a body. Therefore, you are affirming something which is contrary to what is known to you. Likewise, we affirm these Attributes without saying that He has a body; this is the contradiction of the Mu'tazilah. As for the contradiction of those [Al-Asha'irah] who only affirm the Seven Attributes, they say to

[212]اعراض Something nonessential; which can be displayed or appeared only through body

those [Ahl-as-Sunnah wa al-Jama'aat] who affirm the Attributes of Satisfaction, Anger, and so on; Affirming Satisfaction, Anger, Rising over the Throne, Coming down, the Face and Two Hands and so on is considered anthropomorphism, because we do not know anything that is characterized with these Attributes except that it is a body.

Those [Ahl-as-Sunnah wa al-Jama'aat] who affirm all of these Attributes respond to them by saying: you have described Him with the Attributes of Life, Knowledge, Power, Will, Hearing, Seeing and Speech and you know that there is nothing which is described with these characteristics except that it is a body. If our affirmation of these Attributes necessitates anthropomorphism, then your affirmation should also necessitate anthropomorphism. If your affirmation does not imply this, then our affirmation should also not imply this, even if you think it should be implied, because there is no difference between these two situations. However, if you judge differently between them, that would be a contradiction on your part.

Guidelines for Affirmation

We affirm what Allah(سبحانه وتعالى) has affirmed about Himself from attributes of perfection in a manner that is not deficient in any way. Allah(سبحانه وتعالى) says:

﴿...وَلِلَّهِ الْمَثَلُ الأَعْلَىَ وَهُوَ الْعَزِيزُ الْحَكِيمُ﴾[213]

"And for Allah is the highest description. And He is the All-Mighty, the All-Wise."

[213] An-Nahl: 60

The highest description means the most perfect description, unlike anything else.

All of the attributes of Allah(سبحانه وتعالى) are attributes of perfection; whether they are affirmed attributes or negated attributes. It has been established that absolute negation does not apply to Allah(سبحانه وتعالى)'s attributes; the negative attributes are only a means of negating that attribute due to His characterization with its perfect opposite.

For this reason, it is not valid to base the guidelines of affirmation on mere affirmation without resemblance. If that was valid, then it would have been allowed for the fabricator to characterize Allah(سبحانه وتعالى) with any imperfect attribute but while negating resemblance. For example, he would characterize Him with sadness, crying, hunger, thirst and so on – exalted be Allah(سبحانه وتعالى)above all of these shortcomings –while negating any resemblance. He can say: Allah(سبحانه وتعالى)becomes sad but not like the sadness of His slaves; He cries but not like their cry; He becomes hungry but not like their hunger; He feels thirsty but not like their thirst; He eats but not like their eating; just as Allah(سبحانه وتعالى) becomes happy but not like their happiness; He laughs but not like their laughter and He speaks but not like their speech.

Moreover, it would allow the fabricator to affirm many organs for Allah(سبحانه وتعالى)while negating any resemblance. He would say:

Allah(سبحانه وتعالى) has a liver yet unlike His slaves; He has intestines but not like theirs, and so on –Exalted be Allah(سبحانه وتعالى) above all of these. Just as He has a Face but not like theirs and He has two Hands but not like their hands.

The fabricator will say to those who negate these attributes of imperfection but affirm [the attributes of] happiness, laughter, speech, face and two hands: what is the difference between what you have negated and what you have affirmed if you state that mere negation of any resemblance is sufficient for affirmation? I do not violate this guideline; indeed, I affirm these [attributes] while negating any resemblance [to the creation].

If the one who negates says: The difference is the text(i.e. evidence from the Quran and Sunnah).Therefore, whatever is proven by the evidence, I shall affirm it, and whatever is not proven, I shall not affirm it.

Then the fabricator will say: Textual evidence is [a type of] information, and this information is evidence about the informed thing. Additionally, the evidence does not reverse; absence of the evidence does not necessitate the absence of the indicated thing, because it can be proven by another evidence. Therefore, it is possible that what is not proven by textual evidence can still be affirmed at the same time, even if there is no textual evidence. It is well known that the negation of all these attributes has not been mentioned in the text with these special terms. Thus, there is no evidence in negating sadness, crying, hunger, thirst and in negating the liver, stomach and intestine. And since there is no evidence negating it, then it can be affirmed at the same time. Therefore, it is not acceptable to negate it without any evidence. In this way, the one who negates these attributes becomes restricted, since he based his negation solely on negating any resemblance. And it is known that relying on this is not valid. It can only depend on what is proven by the texts and reason from attributes of perfection, in a befitting manner, with no deficiencies. Based on this, whatever is contrary to the Attributes of perfection, then Allah(سبحانه وتعالى) is Exalted. This is because affirming one of two opposites necessitates the negation of the other and its implications.

Based on this argument, it is possible to falsify the characteristics of imperfection proven by the fabricator. It will be said to him: The sadness, crying, hunger, and thirst are attributes of imperfection, which are contrary to the Attributes of perfection. Therefore, they should be negated on behalf of Allah(سبحانه وتعالى). It will also be said: Eating and drinking are kinds of needs, and needs are a shortcoming. And what necessitates a shortcoming is a shortcoming. It will also be said: the liver, stomach and intestines are tools for eating and drinking. Thus, whoever does not need food and drink, will also not need these tools.

As for joy, laughter, anger, and so on, they are attributes of perfection, free of any shortcomings. Therefore, these are not negated on His behalf; yet, they do not resemble the same characteristics of the creation. Glory be to Allah(سبحانه وتعالى), Who has no partner, no opponent or co-equal unto Him. Therefore, it is not permissible for His essence to be like the essence of the creation or that the nature of His Attributes to be like the nature of the characteristics of the creation. This is because He is not a type of creation, neither the angels, nor the human beings, nor the heavens, or the planets, winds, earth and so on.

It is known that for His essence to resemble any of the existing beings is as far from reality as it can be. This is because if two beings are similar, then what is suitable for one should also be suitable for the other, whatever is necessary for one is also necessary for the other, and whatever is inapplicable for one is also inapplicable for the other. Thus, it would be suitable for the Creator, who is a self-existing being, what is suitable for the creation, a created being. It would also necessitate affirming for the creation what is affirmed for the Creator. Thus, the same entity will be both self-existing as well as dependent, existing and non-existing; this would be a contradiction.

◊◊ ◊ ◊◊

The obligation of Believing in al-Qadar (Devine Destiny) and Shari'ah (Islamic Legislation)

A person must have a firm belief in Qadar because it is one of the six pillars of 'Eemân, which fulfills the belief in Allah(سبحانه وتعالى)'s Lordship. It is also a means for achieving true reliance on Allah(سبحانه وتعالى), and entrusting matters to Him, after fulfilling all the valid means. Through it is man's true serenity attained since he knows that whatever befalls him, it could not have been avoided, and whatever does not happen to him, nothing could have made it happen. It eliminates self-admiration at times of achievement since he knows that it has happened only by the decree of Allah(سبحانه وتعالى), and that his action, by which he has achieved his desire, is nothing but means which Allah(سبحانه وتعلى) has facilitated for him. Moreover, it removes anxiety and discontentment at times of loss, failure or misfortune, because he knows that matters are [by the Will] of Allah(سبحانه وتعلى), so he is pleased to submit.

Allah(سبحانه وتعلى) refers to these two issues in His saying:

﴿مَا أَصَابَ مِن مُّصِيبَةٍ فِي الأَرْضِ وَلا فِي أَنفُسِكُمْ إِلاَّ فِي كِتَابٍ مِّن قَبْلِ أَن نَّبْرَأَهَا إِنَّ ذَلِكَ عَلَى اللَّهِ يَسِيرٌ * لِكَيْلا تَأْسَوْا عَلَى مَا فَاتَكُمْ وَلا تَفْرَحُوا بِمَا آتَاكُمْ وَاللَّهُ لا يُحِبُّ كُلَّ مُخْتَالٍ فَخُورٍ﴾[214]

"No calamity befalls on the earth or in yourselves but it is inscribed in the Book of Decrees (AL-Louh Al-Mahfuz) before we bring into existence. Verily, that is easy for Allah. In order that you may not grieve at the things that you feel to get, nor rejoice over that which has been given to you. And Allah likes not every prideful boaster."

[214] Al-Hadeed: 22-23

Man must also have firm belief in the Shari'ah that is brought by the Messengers of Allah, containing His commands and prohibitions, and their consequential rewards or punishments. Thus, he acts in accordance with the commands as well as the prohibitions and he believes in their consequential recompense.

This is because man has free will; therefore, he must be able to act in order to achieve his wishes or avoid what he does not wish. He must also have rules and regulations to control his actions, so as not to fall into harm, or miss what is beneficial, whilst he is unaware. Allah(سبحانه وتعالى)'s legislation, which has been brought by the Messengers, will form these rules and regulation and judge accordingly. It will differentiate between the beneficial and the harmful and between the right and wrong things as well since it is from Allah(سبحانه وتعالى), Who is All-Knower, the Most Merciful, the Most Wise.

Though the intellect can realize the benefits and the harmful in general; yet, the legislation elucidates these matters in details and fully explains it.

We say: Benefit and harm may be known through nature, intellect, or through experiments, or it may be known through legislation. Therefore, the legislation reinforces what has been observed by nature, reason and experience, and likewise, these [nature, reason, experiments] reinforce what has been brought by legislation.

In this issue, people have differed regarding actions, and whether their categorization as good or bad should be based on legislation or intellect?

Analysis: Sometimes, it can be known through legislation or through the intellect, and sometimes through both of them; however, this is from a general perspective. The minute details, however, as well as the knowledge about the consequences of actions in the hereafter, whether of joy or wretchedness and the like, cannot be known without the legislation.

Two groups regarding the issue of Qadar and Shari'ah

Once it is clear that man must have a firm belief in Qadar and Shari'ah, then you should also know that people have divided into two groups regarding this matter:

The First Group: People of guidance and success who believe in Qadar, according to what has been discussed previously about the four stages. They also believe in Shari'ah; thus, they act according to its commandments and prohibitions and believe in their consequential recompense. They do not use Qadar as a justification against the Shari'ah, nor do they use Shari'ah as a justification against Qadar. Moreover, they will never think that these two are contradictory. These are the people of truth who have applied and implemented the following verses in their life:

﴿إِيَّاكَ نَعْبُدُ وَإِيَّاكَ نَسْتَعِينُ﴾[215]

"You (Alone) we worship, and You (Alone) we ask for help (for each and everything)".

They are the believers in line with Allah(سبحانه وتعالى)'s command:

﴿...أَلاَ لَهُ الْخَلْقُ وَالأَمْرُ...﴾[216]

"His is the Creation and Commandment".

[215] Al-Fatihah: 5
[216] Al-A'raf-54

The Second Group: The people of misguidance and condemnation, who oppose the righteous group. They are divided into three sects: Fire Worshipers, Polytheists and Satanists [supporter of Ibliss].

Fire Worshipers [المجوسية]: Qadariyah groups, who believe in the legislation of Allah(سبحانه وتعالى), yet they deny the Qadr. The extremists among them deny the comprehensive knowledge of Allah(سبحانه وتعالى), by saying that:

Allah(سبحانه وتعالى) does not decree the action of man, and He has no knowledge about it before it takes place.

The moderate group among them affirms Allah(سبحانه وتعالى)'s knowledge about actions of man before its occurrence; yet, they deny that the occurrence takes place according to Allah(سبحانه وتعالى)'s will and they said that it is not created by Him. These are the Mu'tazilites and their supporters. Their belief is invalid, according to the previous evidence of the stages of Qadar.

Polytheists [المشركية]: Those who acknowledge the Qadar, yet, they use it as an excuse against the Shari'ah.

As Allah(سبحانه وتعالى) states:

﴿سَيَقُولُ الَّذِينَ أَشْرَكُواْ لَوْ شَاء اللَّهُ مَا أَشْرَكْنَا وَلاَ آبَاؤُنَا وَلاَ حَرَّمْنَا مِن شَيْءٍ كَذَلِكَ كَذَّبَ الَّذِينَ مِن قَبْلِهِم حَتَّى ذَاقُواْ بَأْسَنَا...﴾[217]

"Those who took partners (in worship) with Allah will say: If Allah had willed, we would not have taken partners (in worship) with Him, nor would our fathers, and we would not have forbidden anything (against His Will)".

[217] Al-An'am 148

Satanists [الابليسية]: Those who believe in both Qadr and Shari'ah; yet, they consider these two as a contradiction from Allah(سبحانه وتعالى). Do they challenge the Wisdom of Allah(سبحانه وتعالى) by saying: How can Allah(سبحانه وتعالى) command His servants and forbid them, yet He decrees for them what may be opposing to what He has commanded them with or prohibited them from? Can this be anything but pure contradiction and a conduct inconsistent with wisdom?

These are the followers of Iblees. He argues with Allah(سبحانه وتعالى) when he is commanded to prostrate to Adam by saying:

﴿...أَنَاْ خَيْرٌ مِّنْهُ خَلَقْتَنِي مِن نَّارٍ وَخَلَقْتَهُ مِن طِينٍ﴾[218]

"I am better than him (Adam), You created me from fire, and him You created from clay."

Refuting these two groups has been clarified from the refutation of those who use Qadar as a justification to disobey Allah(سبحانه وتعالى).

Shari'ah

Shari'ah is what has been brought by the Messengers to us about worshiping Allah(سبحانه وتعالى), which is the main purpose behind the creation of Jinn and Mankind.

Allah(سبحانه وتعلى) says:

﴿وَمَا خَلَقْتُ الْجِنَّ وَالإِنسَ إِلاَّ لِيَعْبُدُونِ﴾[219]

---

[218] Al-A'raf: 12
[219] Adh-Dhariyat: 56.

"And I (Allah) created not the jinn and mankind except that they should worship Me (Alone)."

Allah(سبحانه وتعلى) will not accept from anyone any religion other than Islam, Allah(سبحانه وتعلى) says:

﴿وَمَن يَبْتَغِ غَيْرَ الإِسْلاَمِ دِينًا فَلَن يُقْبَلَ مِنْهُ...﴾[220]

"And whoever seeks a religion other than Islam, it will never be accepted of him, and in the Hereafter, he will be one of the losers."

Islam is full submission to Allah(سبحانه وتعلى) by performing His commands and by avoiding His prohibitions, so long as the legislation is operative for every time and place. This is the general meaning of Islam. According to this statement, previous nations are considered Muslims, so long as their laws are operative, not yet substituted or replaced. Allah(سبحانه وتعلى) narrates about Nuh, while he is addressing his people:

﴿فَإِن تَوَلَّيْتُمْ فَمَا سَأَلْتُكُم مِّنْ أَجْرٍ إِنْ أَجْرِيَ إِلاَّ عَلَى اللّهِ وَأُمِرْتُ أَنْ أَكُونَ مِنَ الْمُسْلِمِينَ﴾[221]

"But if you turn away, then no reward have I asked of you; my reward is only from Allah, and I have been commanded to be of the Muslims."

Allah(سبحانه وتعلى) said about Ibrahim:

﴿مَا كَانَ إِبْرَاهِيمُ يَهُودِيًّا وَلاَ نَصْرَانِيًّا وَلَكِن كَانَ حَنِيفًا مُّسْلِمًا وَمَا كَانَ مِنَ الْمُشْرِكِينَ﴾[222]

"Ibrahim (Abraham was neither a Jew nor a Christian, but he was a true Muslim Haneef (Islamic Monotheism – to worship none but Allah(Alone) and he was not of the polytheists."

Allah(سبحانه وتعلى) says:

---

[220] Âli 'Imran: 85.
[221] Yoonus: 72.
[222] Âli 'Imran: 67

﴿إِذْ قَالَ لَهُ رَبُّهُ أَسْلِمْ قَالَ أَسْلَمْتُ لِرَبِّ الْعَالَمِينَ * وَوَصَّى بِهَا إِبْرَاهِيمُ بَنِيهِ وَيَعْقُوبُ يَا بَنِيَّ إِنَّ اللَّهَ اصْطَفَى لَكُمُ الدِّينَ فَلاَ تَمُوتُنَّ إِلاَّ وَأَنتُم مُّسْلِمُونَ﴾[223]

"When his Lord said to him, 'Submit!' He said: I have submitted myself (as a Muslim) to the Lord of the 'Alamen (mankind, jinn and all that exists). And this submission to Allah, Islam, was enjoined by Ibrahim (Abraham) upon his sons and by Ya'qub (Jacob) (saying), "O my sons! Allah has chosen for you the (true) religion, then die not except in the Faith of Islam (as Muslims – Islamic Monotheism)."

Allah(سبحانه وتعلى) narrates about Musa while he is addressing his people:

﴿...يَا قَوْمِ إِن كُنتُمْ آمَنتُم بِاللَّهِ فَعَلَيْهِ تَوَكَّلُواْ إِن كُنتُم مُّسْلِمِينَ﴾[224]

"And Moses said: 'O my people! If you have believed in Allah, then put your trust in Him if you are Muslims (those who submit to Allah's Will).'"

Allah(سبحانه وتعلى) describes the Torah:

﴿إِنَّا أَنزَلْنَا التَّوْرَاةَ فِيهَا هُدًى وَنُورٌ يَحْكُمُ بِهَا النَّبِيُّونَ الَّذِينَ أَسْلَمُواْ لِلَّذِينَ هَادُواْ...﴾[225]

"Verily, We did send down the Tawrâh (Torah), therein was guidance and light, by which the Prophets, who submitted themselves to Allah's Will, judged for the Jews."

Allah(سبحانه وتعلى) says about followers of 'Isaa:

﴿وَإِذْ أَوْحَيْتُ إِلَى الْحَوَارِيِّينَ أَنْ آمِنُواْ بِي وَبِرَسُولِي قَالُواْ آمَنَّا وَاشْهَدْ بِأَنَّنَا مُسْلِمُونَ﴾[226]

---

[223] Al-Baqarah: 131-132.
[224] Yoonus: 84
[225] Al-Ma'idah-44
[226] Al-Ma'idah-111

"And when I (Allah) revealed to Al-Hawaariyyeen [the disciples of 'Isaa (Jesus)] to believe in Me and My Messenger, they said: 'We believe. And bear witness that we are Muslims.'"

Allah(سبحانه وتعلى) says about Queen of Saba:

﴿...رَبِّ إِنِّي ظَلَمْتُ نَفْسِي وَأَسْلَمْتُ مَعَ سُلَيْمَانَ لِلَّهِ رَبِّ الْعَالَمِينَ﴾[227]

"She said: 'My Lord! Verily, I have wronged myself, and I submit in Islam, together with Sulaimaan (Solomon) to Allah, the Lord of the 'Alamen (mankind, jinn and all that exists).'"

As for the conventional meaning of Islam, it refers to the legislation that has been brought by Muhammad ﷺ, Allah(سبحانه وتعلى) says:

﴿قُلْ إِنَّ صَلاتِي وَنُسُكِي وَمَحْيَايَ وَمَمَاتِي لِلَّهِ رَبِّ الْعَالَمِينَ * لاَ شَرِيكَ لَهُ وَبِذَلِكَ أُمِرْتُ وَأَنَاْ أَوَّلُ الْمُسْلِمِينَ﴾[228]

"Say (O Muhammad: Verily, my Salat (prayer), my sacrifice, my living, and my dying are for Allah, the Lord of the worlds (mankind, jinn and all that exists). He has no partner, and of this, I have been commanded, and I am the first of the Muslims."

Allah(سبحانه وتعلى) says about his followers:

﴿...هُوَ سَمَّاكُمُ الْمُسْلِمِينَ مِن قَبْلُ وَفِي هَذَا لِيَكُونَ الرَّسُولُ شَهِيدًا عَلَيْكُمْ...﴾[229]

"It is He (Allah) Who has named you as Muslims both before and in this (the Qur'an), that the Messenger may be a witness over you…."

[227] An-Naml: 44
[228] Al-An'am: 162-163
[229] Al-Hajj: 78

However, after the prophethood of Muhammad ﷺ, there is no acceptable Islam except by following him. This is because his religion supersedes other religions, and his Shari'ah annuls all other previous legislation. Allah(سبحانه وتعلى) says:

﴿وَإِذْ أَخَذَ اللَّهُ مِيثَاقَ النَّبِيِّينَ لَمَا آتَيْتُكُم مِّن كِتَابٍ وَحِكْمَةٍ ثُمَّ جَاءَكُمْ رَسُولٌ مُّصَدِّقٌ لِّمَا مَعَكُمْ لَتُؤْمِنُنَّ بِهِ وَلَتَنصُرُنَّهُ قَالَ أَأَقْرَرْتُمْ وَأَخَذْتُمْ عَلَى ذَلِكُمْ إِصْرِي قَالُواْ أَقْرَرْنَا قَالَ فَاشْهَدُواْ وَأَنَاْ مَعَكُم مِّنَ الشَّاهِدِينَ﴾[230]

"And (remember) when Allah took the Covenant of the Prophets, (saying): " Take whatever I gave you from the Book and Hikmah (understanding of the Laws of Allah, and afterwards there will come to you a Messenger confirming what is with you; you must, then believe in him and help him." (Allah) said: "Do you agree (to it) and will take up My Covenant (Which I conclude with you)?" They said: "We agree." He said: "Then bear witness, and I am with you among the witnesses (for this)."

The Shari'ahs before him confirm the prophethood of Muhammad ﷺ, as Allah(سبحانه وتعلى) says:

﴿وَأَنزَلْنَا إِلَيْكَ الْكِتَابَ بِالْحَقِّ مُصَدِّقًا لِّمَا بَيْنَ يَدَيْهِ مِنَ الْكِتَابِ وَمُهَيْمِنًا عَلَيْهِ...﴾[231]

"And when we have sent down to you the Books (this Qur'an) in truth, confirming the Scriptures (Books) that came before it and Muhaiminan (trustworthy in highness and a witness) over it (old Scriptures)."

Allah(سبحانه وتعلى) says:

﴿هُوَ الَّذِي أَرْسَلَ رَسُولَهُ بِالْهُدَى وَدِينِ الْحَقِّ لِيُظْهِرَهُ عَلَى الدِّينِ كُلِّهِ...﴾[232]

---

[230] Âli 'Imran: 81
[231] Al-Ma'idah: 48
[232] At-Tawbah: 33

"It is He Who has sent His Messenger (Muhammad) with guidance and the religion of truth (Islam), to make it superior over all religions."

Here, the superiority is for its honor as well as for its laws.

Whoever receives the message of Prophet Muhammad ﷺ and then neither believes in him nor follows him, then he will not be considered as a believer in God or as a Muslim, rather he is an infidel and will be condemned to the hell-fire. Prophet ﷺ says: "By Him in Whose hand is the life of Muhammad, he who amongst the community of Jews or Christians hears about me, but does not affirm his belief in that with which I have been sent and dies in the state (of disbelief), he shall be one of the denizens of Hell-Fire."[233] This Hadith is reported in Muslim on the authority of Abu Hurayrah رضي الله عنه.

Thus, it is clear that the dispute over regarding the previous nations as Muslim or not is simply a verbal dispute. Indeed, Islam, in the general sense, encompasses all the established Shari'ah, which Allah(سبحانه وتعلى) has sent with every prophet; thus, it represents the submission of every nation that follows their prophets, so long as the legislation of that prophet remains operative, and has not been annulled, according to the consensus of the scholars and the aforementioned evidence. However, after the prophethood of Muhammad ﷺ, Islam specifically refers to what he has come with; thus, whoever does not believe in him and does not follow him, and then he will not be considered as a Muslim.

Moreover, whoever claims that there are other recognized religions, which is acceptable in the sight of Allah(سبحانه وتعلى), beside Islam such as Judaism, Christianity and so on, he will be considered as a liar, as Allah(سبحانه وتعلى) says:

233 Sahih Muslim, Chapter of Eemân; the Obligation of believing in our Prophet Muhammad (saws), on the authority of Abu Hurayrah.

﴿إِنَّ الدِّينَ عِندَ اللَّهِ الإِسْلَامُ...﴾[234]

"Truly, the religion with Allah is Islam.

Allah(سبحانه وتعلى) also says:

﴿وَمَن يَبْتَغِ غَيْرَ الإِسْلَامِ دِينًا فَلَن يُقْبَلَ مِنْهُ وَهُوَ فِي الآخِرَةِ مِنَ الْخَاسِرِينَ﴾[235]

"And whoever seeks a religion other than Islam, it will never be accepted of him, and in the Hereafter, he will be one of the losers."

Additionally, if Islam means to follow the existing legislation, then, if some portions become abrogated, the abrogated portion will no longer be considered part of the religion, nor will it be considered as Islam. For example, facing Baitil Maqdis used to be an Islamic ruling, before it was abrogated. However, after abrogation, Baitul Maqdis is no longer Qibla, and thus following that rule will no longer be considered part of the religion nor will it be considered Islam. Visiting the graves used to be an un-Islamic ritual while it was prohibited; however, later o,n when it was encouraged to do so, it became part of the Islamic Shari'ah [legislation].

Tawheed ar-Rububiyah

Islam is founded upon Tawheed(Oneness of Allah(سبحانه وتعلى)), Allah(سبحانه وتعلى) says:

﴿قُلْ إِنَّمَا يُوحَى إِلَيَّ أَنَّمَا إِلَهُكُمْ إِلَهٌ وَاحِدٌ فَهَلْ أَنتُم مُّسْلِمُونَ﴾[236]

234 Âli 'Imran: 19
235 Âli 'Imran: 85
236 Al-Anbiya':108

"Say: it is revealed to me that your Ilaah (God) is only one Ilaah (God-Allah). Will you then submit to His Will (become Muslims and worshiping others besides Allah)?"

Tawheed should consist of affirmation and negation, because mere negation is a suspension, and mere affirmation does not negate association. Therefore, Tawheed is not complete with both affirmation and negation.

Scholars have categorized al-Tawheed – through research and analysis – into three types:

The First Type: Tawheed ar-Rububiyah. (The Oneness of the Lordship of Allah(سبحانه وتعلى)) The Oneness of the Divinity

The Second Type: **Tawheed al-Uluhiyah** [al-Ebadah] (The Oneness of the Worship of Allah(سبحانه وتعلى))

The Third Type: **Tawheed al-Asma was-Sifat** (The Oneness/the Uniqueness of the Names and Attributes of Allah(سبحانه وتعلى)).

Allah(سبحانه وتعلى) has described these three categories in the following verse:

﴿رَبُّ السَّمَاوَاتِ وَالأَرْضِ وَمَا بَيْنَهُمَا فَاعْبُدْهُ وَاصْطَبِرْ لِعِبَادَتِهِ هَلْ تَعْلَمُ لَهُ سَمِيًّا﴾[237]

"The Lord of the Heavens and the earth, and all that is between them, so worship Him (alone) and be constant and patient in His worship. Do you know of any who is similar to Him?"

Tawheed ar-Rububiyah: (The Oneness of the Lordship of Allah (سبحانه وتعلى)) means that there is only one God (Allah(سبحانه وتعلى)), Who is the sole Creator of all creation, Sustainer of the whole Universe.

[237] Maryam:65

As Allah(سبحانه وتعلى) says:

﴿...أَلاَ لَهُ الْخَلْقُ وَالأَمْرُ تَبَارَكَ اللَّهُ رَبُّ الْعَالَمِينَ﴾[238]

"Surely, His is the Creation and Commandment. Blessed is Allah, the Lord of the 'Alameen (mankind, jinn and all that exists)!

And He(سبحانه وتعلى) says:

﴿وَلِلَّهِ مُلْكُ السَّمَاوَاتِ وَالأَرْضِ وَاللَّهُ عَلَىَ كُلِّ شَيْءٍ قَدِيرٌ﴾[239]

"And to Allah belongs the dominion of the heavens and the earth, and Allah has power over all things."

Allah(سبحانه وتعلى) says:

﴿قُلِ ادْعُوا الَّذِينَ زَعَمْتُم مِّن دُونِ اللَّهِ لا يَمْلِكُونَ مِثْقَالَ ذَرَّةٍ فِي السَّمَاوَاتِ وَلا فِي الأَرْضِ وَمَا لَهُمْ فِيهِمَا مِن شِرْكٍ وَمَا لَهُ مِنْهُم مِّن ظَهِيرٍ * وَلا تَنفَعُ الشَّفَاعَةُ عِندَهُ إِلاَّ لِمَنْ أَذِنَ لَهُ...﴾[240]

"Say: (O Muhammad) Call upon those whom you assert (to be associate gods) besides Allah, they possess not even an atom's (or small ant's) weight either in the heavens or on the earth, nor have they any share in either, nor there is for Him any supporter from among them. Intercession with Him profits not except for him whom He permits."

This type of Tawheed was acknowledged by the polytheists among whom Allah(سبحانه وتعلى) has sent His Messenger ﷺ, as Allah(سبحانه وتعلى) says:

﴿وَلَئِن سَأَلْتَهُم مَّنْ خَلَقَهُمْ لَيَقُولُنَّ اللَّهُ...﴾[241]

[238] Al-A'raf: 54
[239] Âli 'Imran:189
[240] Saba: 22-23

"And if you ask them who created them, they will surely say: "Allah".

And Allah(سبحانه وتعلى) says:

﴿وَلَئِن سَأَلْتَهُم مَّنْ خَلَقَ السَّمَاوَاتِ وَالأَرْضَ لَيَقُولُنَّ اللَّهُ...﴾[242]

"And if you (O Muhammad) ask them: "Who has created the heavens and the earth, they will certainly say: "Allah"."

Allah(سبحانه وتعلى) says:

﴿قُلْ مَن يَرْزُقُكُم مِّنَ السَّمَاء وَالأَرْضِ أَمَّن يَمْلِكُ السَّمْعَ وَالأَبْصَارَ وَمَن يُخْرِجُ الْحَيَّ مِنَ الْمَيِّتِ
وَيُخْرِجُ الْمَيِّتَ مِنَ الْحَيِّ وَمَن يُدَبِّرُ الأَمْرَ فَسَيَقُولُونَ اللَّهُ...﴾[243]

"Say (O Muhammad): Who provides for you from the sky and the earth? Or who owns hearing and sight? And who brings out the living from the dead and brings out the dead from the living? And who disposes the affairs? They will say: "Allah"."

Allah(سبحانه وتعلى) says:

﴿قُل لِّمَنِ الأَرْضُ وَمَن فِيهَا إِن كُنتُمْ تَعْلَمُونَ * سَيَقُولُونَ لِلَّهِ قُلْ أَفَلا تَذَكَّرُونَ * قُلْ مَن رَّبُّ
السَّمَاوَاتِ السَّبْعِ وَرَبُّ الْعَرْشِ الْعَظِيمِ * سَيَقُولُونَ لِلَّهِ قُلْ أَفَلا تَتَّقُونَ * قُلْ مَن بِيَدِهِ مَلَكُوتُ كُلِّ
شَيْءٍ وَهُوَ يُجِيرُ وَلا يُجَارُ عَلَيْهِ إِن كُنتُمْ تَعْلَمُونَ * سَيَقُولُونَ لِلَّهِ قُلْ فَأَنَّى تُسْحَرُونَ * بَلْ
أَتَيْنَاهُم بِالْحَقِّ وَإِنَّهُمْ لَكَاذِبُونَ﴾[244]

"Say: 'Whose is the earth and whosoever is therein? If you know!'

They will say: 'It is Allah's!' Say: 'Will you not then remember?'

[241] Zukhruf: 87
[242] Luqman: 25
[243] Yoonus: 31
[244] Al-Mu'minoon: 84-90

Say: 'Who is (the) Lord of the seven heavens, and (the) Lord of the Great Throne?'

They will say: 'Allah'. Say: 'Will you not then fear Allah (believe in His Oneness, obey Him, believe in the Resurrection and Recompense for each and every good or bad deed).'

Say: 'In Whose Hand is the sovereignty of everything (i.e. treasures of each and everything)? And He protects (all), while against Whom there is no protector, (i.e. if Allah saves anyone none can punish or harm him, and if Allah punishes or harms anyone none can save him), if you know.' [Tafsir Al-Qurtubi, Vol. 12, Page 145]

They will say: '(All that belongs) to Allah.' Say: 'How then are you deceived and turn away from the truth?'

Nay, but We have brought them the truth (Islamic Monotheism), and verily, they (disbelievers) are liars."

Neither those polytheists nor others, who have believed in the creator, assume that there is a partner beside Allah(سبحانه وتعلى) who assists Him in the creation of heavens and earth, nor do they assume there are two creators who are same in attributes and actions. Moreover, [such practices] has also not been mentioned by any historian, who studies beliefs and religious views.

Historians, however, have reported about Zoroastrianism who believes in two beings: the light and the darkness. They believe that the light has created the beneficial things while the darkness has created the harmful things. However, they do not deem these two beings the same in power and action; indeed, the light illuminates and goes in line with the natural instinct while darkness does not.

According to them, light is eternal and they have two opinions about the darkness:

The First Opinion: The darkness is Muhdath [brought into existence] and the light has created it; therefore, the light is more perfect than the darkness.

The Second Opinion: It is eternal but it does not create anything except bad.

Thus, the darkness is imperfect in its actions, as compared to the light, as it is less perfect than light in its existence and qualities. As for the statement of Pharaoh towards his nations during their gathering:

﴿فَقَالَ أَنَا رَبُّكُمُ الأَعْلَى﴾[245]

"Saying: 'I am your lord, most high'

And his statement:

﴿...يَا أَيُّهَا الْمَلأُ مَا عَلِمْتُ لَكُم مِّنْ إِلَهٍ غَيْرِي ...﴾[246]

"O chiefs! I know not that you have an ilah (a god) other than me."

These arrogant statements do not stem from his belief; in fact, he has acknowledged deeply within himself that Allah(سبحانه وتعلى) is indeed The Sustainer of heavens and earth. That is why he does not deny Musa's statement when he says:

﴿قَالَ لَقَدْ عَلِمْتَ مَا أَنزَلَ هَؤُلاء إِلاَّ رَبُّ السَّمَاوَاتِ وَالأَرْضِ بَصَائِرَ وَإِنِّي لأَظُنُّكَ يَا فِرْعَوْنُ مَثْبُورًا﴾[247]

"[Musa (Moses)] said: 'Verily, you know that these signs have been sent down by none but the Lord of the heavens and the earth as clear (evidence i.e. proofs of Allah's Oneness and His Omnipotence, etc.).

[245] An-Nazi'at: 24
[246] Al-Qasas: 38
[247] Al-Isra': 102

And I think you are, indeed, O Fir'aun (Pharaoh) doomed to destruction (away from all good)!'"

Allah(سبحانه وتعالى) says about Pharaoh and his nation:

﴿وَجَحَدُوا بِهَا وَاسْتَيْقَنَتْهَا أَنفُسُهُمْ ظُلْمًا وَعُلُوًّا فَانظُرْ كَيْفَ كَانَ عَاقِبَةُ الْمُفْسِدِينَ﴾[248]

"And they belied them (those Ayat) wrongfully and arrogantly, though their ownselves were convinced thereof [i.e. those (Ayat) are from Allah, and Musa (Moses) is the Messenger of Allah in truth, but they disliked to obey Musa (Moses) and hated to believe in his Message of Monotheism]. So see what was the end of the Mufsidun (disbelievers, disobedient to Allah, evil-doers, liars.)."

As for the statement of some people, who say, some events are created by other than Allah(سبحانه وتعالى), such as al-Qadariyah, who say that man's actions are created by himself. They acknowledge that humans are created; Allah(سبحانه وتعالى) has created them as well as their power.

Likewise, the philosophers, naturalists and astrologists think that some creatures have innovative powers, and they believe that these events are created and have been brought into existence.

By these above statements, it is established that nobody has ever claimed that there are two equal creators for the universe.

[248] An-Naml: 14

Tawheed al-Uluhiyah

Tawheed al-Uluhiyah [al-Ebadah] (The Oneness of the Worship of Allah(سبحانه وتعلى)): means to single out Allah(سبحانه وتعلى) in worship; that no one but Allah(سبحانه وتعلى) alone is worthy of sincere worship and no one has the right to be worshipped except Him, neither an angel, nor a messenger, a prophet, a wali (Muslim saint), a tree, a stone, sun, moon or anything else.

Evidence of this Tawheed is: Allah(سبحانه وتعلى) says:

﴿وَاعْبُدُواْ اللّهَ وَلاَ تُشْرِكُواْ بِهِ شَيْئًا...﴾[249]

"Worship Allah and join none with Him (in worship)."

Allah(سبحانه وتعلى) says:

﴿وَمَا أَرْسَلْنَا مِن قَبْلِكَ مِن رَّسُولٍ إِلاَّ نُوحِي إِلَيْهِ أَنَّهُ لا إِلَهَ إِلاَّ أَنَا فَاعْبُدُونِ﴾[250]

"And We did not send any Messenger before you but We revealed to Him (saying): None has the right to be worshiped but I (Allah), so worship Me (Alone and none else)."

Allah(سبحانه وتعلى) says:

﴿وَإِلَـهُكُمْ إِلَهٌ وَاحِدٌ لاَّ إِلَهَ إِلاَّ هُوَ الرَّحْمَنُ الرَّحِيمُ﴾[251]

"And your Ilaah (God) is One Ilaah (God-Allah), Laa ilaaha illa Huwa (there is none who has the right to be worshiped but He) the Most Gracious, the Most Merciful."

Allah(سبحانه وتعلى) says:

[249] Al-Nisa': 36
[250] Al-Anbiya': 25
[251] Al-Baqarah: 163

﴿شَهِدَ اللَّهُ أَنَّهُ لاَ إِلَهَ إِلاَّ هُوَ وَالْمَلاَئِكَةُ وَأُوْلُواْ الْعِلْمِ قَائِمًا بِالْقِسْطِ لاَ إِلَهَ إِلاَّ هُوَ الْعَزِيزُ الْحَكِيمُ﴾[252]

"Allah bears witness that Laa ilaaha illa Huwa (there is none who has the right to be worshiped but He), and the angels, and those having knowledge (also give this witness); (He always maintains His creation in Justice. Laa ilaaha illa Huwa (there is none who has the right to be worshiped but He), the All-Mighty, the All-Wise."

This type of Tawheed has been neglected by the polytheists among whom Allah(سبحانه وتعلى) has sent His messenger ﷺ.

Allah(سبحانه وتعلى) says:

﴿إِنَّهُمْ كَانُوا إِذَا قِيلَ لَهُمْ لا إِلَهَ إِلاَّ اللَّهُ يَسْتَكْبِرُونَ * وَيَقُولُونَ أَئِنَّا لَتَارِكُوا آلِهَتِنَا لِشَاعِرٍ مَّجْنُونٍ﴾[253]

"Truly, when it was said to them: 'Laa ilaaha illAllah (none has the right to be worshiped but Allah),' They puffed themselves up with pride. And (they) said, 'Are we going to abandon our aalihah (gods) for the sake of a mad poet?'"

And Allah(سبحانه وتعلى) says:

﴿وَعَجِبُوا أَن جَاءَهُم مُّنذِرٌ مِّنْهُمْ وَقَالَ الْكَافِرُونَ هَذَا سَاحِرٌ كَذَّابٌ * أَجَعَلَ الآلِهَةَ إِلَهًا وَاحِدًا إِنَّ هَذَا لَشَيْءٌ عُجَابٌ *وَانطَلَقَ الْمَلأُ مِنْهُمْ أَنِ امْشُوا وَاصْبِرُوا عَلَى آلِهَتِكُمْ إِنَّ هَذَا لَشَيْءٌ يُرَادُ﴾[254]

"And they (Arab pagans) wonder that a warner (Prophet Muhammad) has come to them from among themselves! And the disbelievers say: "This (Prophet Muhammad) is a sorcerer, a liar. 'Has he made the aliha (gods) (all) into One Ilah (God - Allah). Verily, this is a curious thing!' And the leaders among them went about (saying): 'Go on, and remain

[252] Ali 'Imran: 18
[253] As-Saffat: 35-36
[254] Sad: 4-6

constant to your aliha (gods)! Verily, This is a thing designed (against you)!'"

Due to their rejection, the Prophet ﷺ fought against them and legalized their blood, wealth, and permitted taking their wives and children as slaves, by Allah(سبحانه وتعلى)'s command. Their acknowledgement of the Lordship of Allah(سبحانه وتعلى) was not sufficient to excuse them from Shirk and was not sufficient to safeguard their blood and wealth.

The implementation of this type of Tawheed is to worship Allah(سبحانه وتعلى), without associating any partner to Him, by following the legislation that has been brought by the Allah(سبحانه وتعلى)'s Messengers. As Allah(سبحانه وتعلى) says:

﴿...فَمَن كَانَ يَرْجُو لِقَاء رَبِّهِ فَلْيَعْمَلْ عَمَلا صَالِحًا وَلا يُشْرِكْ بِعِبَادَةِ رَبِّهِ أَحَدًا﴾[255]

"So whoever hopes for the Meeting with his Lord, let him work righteousness and associate none as a partner in the worship of his Lord."

Therefore, whoever does not worship Allah(سبحانه وتعلى), he is arrogant and not a monotheist. Whoever worships Him while associating partners, and then he is a polytheist. And whoever worships Him without following His legislation, then he is an innovator, whose Tawheed is imperfect because he has associated a partner with Allah(سبحانه وتعلى) in legislating.

'Ibâdah (worship) has two meanings:

- Worship, which is the action of the slave; it is to humble oneself to the One Worshipped out of love and respect. These two matters (love and respect) are the pillars of 'Ibaadah; due to this love, the slave will do whatever he is commanded to do to please

[255] Al-Kahf: 110

his Lord and due to His respect, the slave will stay away from the prohibited things which may cause His anger.

- The action itself, which includes all actions through which the slave worships his Lord. Cleanliness, prayer, charity, fasting, pilgrimage, obedience towards parents, keeping ties of kinship, and so on, are some types of 'Ibâdah.

'Ibâdah has two conditions:

- Sincerity in worship; so that it is done only for the sake of Allah(سبحانه وتعلى) and to attain the highest status in [paradise]. This is from the fruits of implementing the Shahadah (Laa ilaha illa Allah) [That none is worthy of being worshipped except Allah(سبحانه وتعلى)].
- Following the Prophet ﷺ, so that worshipping Allah(سبحانه وتعلى) is not done except by following what he has legislated. This is from the fruits of implementing the [second part of the] Shahadah, that Mohammad ﷺ is the Messenger of Allah(سبحانه وتعلى).

Thus, the worship of the polytheists is not accepted and is invalid because it is missing the first condition. And the worship of the innovators is not accepted and is invalid because it is missing the second condition. These two conditions of 'Ibaadah have been established by the Book of Allah(سبحانه وتعلى) as well as by the Sunnah of the Prophet ﷺ .

The Evidence for Ikhlaas (sincerity) from the Qur'an:

Allah(سبحانه وتعلى) says:

﴿إِنَّا أَنزَلْنَا إِلَيْكَ الْكِتَابَ بِالْحَقِّ فَاعْبُدِ اللَّهَ مُخْلِصًا لَّهُ الدِّينَ *أَلا لِلَّهِ الدِّينُ الْخَالِصُ وَالَّذِينَ اتَّخَذُوا مِن دُونِهِ أَوْلِيَاءَ مَا نَعْبُدُهُمْ إِلاَّ لِيُقَرِّبُونَا إِلَى اللَّهِ زُلْفَى إِنَّ اللَّهَ يَحْكُمُ بَيْنَهُمْ فِي مَا هُمْ فِيهِ يَخْتَلِفُونَ إِنَّ اللَّهَ لا يَهْدِي مَنْ هُوَ كَاذِبٌ كَفَّارٌ﴾[256]

"Verily, We have sent down the Book to you (O Muhammad) in truth: So worship Allah (Alone) by doing religious deeds sincerely for Allah's sake only, (and not to show-off, and not to set up rivals with Him in worship). Surely, the religion (i.e. the worship and the obedience) is for Allah only. And those who take Auliya' (protectors and helpers) besides Him (say): 'We worship them only that they may bring us near to Allah.' Verily, Allah will judge between them concerning that wherein they differ. Truly, Allah guides not him who is a liar, and a disbeliever."

And Allah(سبحانه وتعلى) says:

﴿وَمَا أُمِرُوا إِلاَّ لِيَعْبُدُوا اللَّهَ مُخْلِصِينَ لَهُ الدِّينَ حُنَفَاء...﴾[257]

"And they were commanded not, but that they should worship Allah, and worship none but Him Alone (abstaining from ascribing partners to Him), and perform As-Salat (Iqamat-as-Salat) and give Zakat: and that is the right religion."

And Allah(سبحانه وتعلى) says:

﴿...وَلَوْ أَشْرَكُواْ لَحَبِطَ عَنْهُم مَّا كَانُواْ يَعْمَلُونَ﴾[258]

"But if they had joined in worship others with Allah (سبحانه وتعلى), all that they used to do would have been of no benefit to them."

And many other verses which bear the proofs for Ikhlaas (sincerity).

---

[256] Az-Zumar: 2-3
[257] Al-Bayyinah: 5
[258] Al-An'am: 88

The Evidence for Ikhlaas (sincerity) from the Sunnah of the Prophet ﷺ:

It has been collected by Imâm Bukhari and Muslim: It is narrated on the authority of 'Umar ibn al-Khattaab ؓ, who says: I have heard the Prophet ﷺ say, "O people! The reward of deeds depends upon the intentions, and every person will get the reward according to what he has intended. So, whosoever emigrates for Allah(سبحانه وتعلى) and His Messenger ﷺ, then his emigration will be for Allah(سبحانه وتعلى) and His Messenger, and whosoever emigrates to take the worldly benefit or for a woman to marry, then his emigration will be for what he emigrated for."[259] This is one of the sentences of Bukhari.

And in Sahih Muslim, it is reported by Abu Hurayrah ؓ that Allah's Messenger ﷺ states: "Allah, the Most High and Exalted, says: 'I am the One who does not stand in need of a partner. If anyone does anything in which he associates anyone else with Me, I shall abandon him with one whom he associates with Allah.'"[260]

The Evidence for Following the Prophet ﷺ from the Qur'an:

Allah(سبحانه وتعلى) says:

﴿وَأَنَّ هَذَا صِرَاطِي مُسْتَقِيمًا فَاتَّبِعُوهُ وَلاَ تَتَّبِعُواْ السُّبُلَ فَتَفَرَّقَ بِكُمْ عَن سَبِيلِهِ...﴾[261]

---

[259] Sahih Al-Bukhari, the book of tricks, chapter: avoiding the use of tricks. And everybody will get (the reward) according to his intention in taking oaths and other things, *Hadith* no: 6953, Sahih Muslim, the book of Jihaad, chapter: the Prophets saying: the rewards depend upon the intentions, *Hadith* no: 1907.

[260] Sahih Muslim, book of pertaining to piety and softening of hearts, chapter: He who associates one as an object of worship with Allah in his deeds, *Hadith* no: 2985.

[261] Al-An'am: 153

"And verily, this (i.e. Allah's Commandments) is my Straight Path, so follow it, and follow not (other) paths, for they will separate you away from His Path."

Allah(سبحانه وتعلى) says:

﴿وَمَن يَبْتَغِ غَيْرَ الإِسْلاَمِ دِينًا فَلَن يُقْبَلَ مِنْهُ وَهُوَ فِي الآخِرَةِ مِنَ الْخَاسِرِينَ﴾[262]

"And whoever seeks a religion other than Islam, it will never be accepted of him, and in the Hereafter, he will be one of the losers."

Allah(سبحانه وتعلى) says about the description of

the Prophet ﷺ:

﴿...فَالَّذِينَ آمَنُواْ بِهِ وَعَزَّرُوهُ وَنَصَرُوهُ وَاتَّبَعُواْ النُّورَ الَّذِيَ أُنزِلَ مَعَهُ أُوْلَئِكَ هُمُ الْمُفْلِحُونَ﴾[263]

"So those who believe in him (Muhammad), honor him, help him, and follow the light (the Qur'an) which has been sent down with him, it is they who will be successful."

And many other verses which bear the proof of following Prophetic Narrations.

The Evidence from the Sunnah about Following the Prophet ﷺ:

Imâm Bukhari and Muslim have compiled in their books on the authority of A'ishah رضي الله عنها that the Prophet said: "He who innovates things in our affairs for which there is no valid (reason) (commits sin) and these are to be rejected."

262 Ali 'Imran: 85
263 Al-A'raf: 157

In Sahih Muslim, it is reported on the authority of Jabir ibn Abdullah ﷺ that the Messenger of Allah(سبحانه وتعلى), while delivering the sermon to the people on Friday would say: "Indeed, and the best of the talks is embodied in the book of Allah(سبحانه وتعلى), and the best of the guidance is the guidance given by Muhammad ﷺ. And the most evil of affairs are their innovations, and every innovation is an error."

It is also authentically reported by Jabir ﷺ that the Prophet ﷺ says: "He among you who lives long enough after me will see many differences. So for you is to observe my Sunnah and the Sunnah of the rightly guided Caliphs, holding on to them with your molar teeth. Beware of matters newly introduced, for every innovation (bid'ah) is an error, and every innovation (bid'ah) is astray."[264] (Narrated by Imâm Ahmad and Abu Dawud also)

Adherence [to the Prophet ﷺ] cannot be fulfilled except by ascertaining that worship is performed in line with the Shari'ah; in its motive, type, quantity, method, time and place.

Worship has many types:

Among these types are **prayer and sacrifice**, as Allah(سبحانه وتعلى) says:

﴿فَصَلِّ لِرَبِّكَ وَانْحَرْ﴾[265]

"Therefore turn in prayer to your Lord and sacrifice (to Him only)."

Allah(سبحانه وتعلى) says:

﴿قُلْ إِنَّ صَلاتِي وَنُسُكِي وَمَحْيَايَ وَمَمَاتِي لِلَّهِ رَبِّ الْعَالَمِينَ * لاَ شَرِيكَ لَهُ وَبِذَلِكَ أُمِرْتُ وَأَنَاْ أَوَّلُ الْمُسْلِمِينَ﴾[266]

[264] Ahmad: (4/126,127). Abu Dawud: (4607). At-Tirmidhi: (2676). Ibn Majah: (42,43).
[265] Al-Kawthar: 2

"Say (O Muhammad: Verily, my Salat (prayer), my sacrifice, my living, and my dying are for Allah, the Lord of the worlds (mankind, jinn and all that exists). He has no partner, and of this, I have been commanded, and I am the first of the Muslims."

So whoever prays for other than Allah(سبحانه وتعلى), he will be considered as a polytheist, and whoever sacrifices before other than Allah(سبحانه وتعلى), seeking closeness and out of veneration, he will be considered as a polytheist.

Tawakkul :(putting trust in Allah (سبحانه وتعلى)): Allah(سبحانه وتعلى) says:

﴿...وَعَلَى اللَّهِ فَتَوَكَّلُوٓاْ إِن كُنتُم مُّؤْمِنِينَ﴾[267]

"And put your trust in Allah if you are believers indeed."

Allah(سبحانه وتعلى) says:

﴿...فَاعْبُدْهُ وَتَوَكَّلْ عَلَيْهِ...﴾[268]

"So worship Him (O Muhammad) and put your trust in Him."

And since Tawakkul is special to Allah(سبحانه وتعلى), then He alone is sufficient for His slaves, as Allah(سبحانه وتعلى) says:

﴿...وَمَن يَتَوَكَّلْ عَلَى اللَّهِ فَهُوَ حَسْبُهُ إِنَّ اللَّهَ بَالِغُ أَمْرِهِ...﴾[269]

"And whosoever puts his trust in Allah, then He will suffice him. Verily, Allah will accomplish his purpose."

As for His saying:

---

[266] Al-An'am: 162-163
[267] Al-Ma'idah: 23
[268] Hood: 123
[269] At-Talaq: 3

﴿يَا أَيُّهَا النَّبِيُّ حَسْبُكَ اللَّهُ وَمَنِ اتَّبَعَكَ مِنَ الْمُؤْمِنِينَ﴾[270]

"O Prophet (Muhammad)! Allah is Sufficient for you and for the believers who follow you."

Here, the meaning is that Allah(سبحانه وتعلى) is enough for you (Muhammad ﷺ) as well as sufficient for the believers. The saying: ﴿وَمَنِ اتَّبَعَكَ﴾, it is connected to the "ك" in ﴿حَسْبُكَ﴾ not connected to "الله" as some people may mistake it so. Indeed, this alters the real meaning, so in turn, it would be: Allah(سبحانه وتعلى) and the believers are sufficient for the Prophet ﷺ, which is incorrect. Indeed, the status of the Prophet ﷺ is higher than the believers, so it would be illogical for the Prophet ﷺ to depend on his followers who are holding the lower status.

Khashyah or Khawf [Fear of Allah(سبحانه وتعلى)]: seeking Fear of Allah(سبحانه وتعلى) through the worship of HIM(سبحانه وتعلى) and His closeness. As Allah(سبحانه وتعلى) says:

﴿إِنَّمَا ذَلِكُمُ الشَّيْطَانُ يُخَوِّفُ أَوْلِيَاءهُ فَلاَ تَخَافُوهُمْ وَخَافُونِ إِن كُنتُم مُّؤْمِنِينَ﴾[271]

"It is only Shaitan (Satan) that suggests to you the fear of his Auliya' [supporters and friends (polytheists, disbelievers in the Oneness of Allah and in His Messenger (Muhammad)], so fear them not, but fear Me, if you are (true) believers."

Allah(سبحانه وتعلى) says:

﴿...فَلاَ تَخْشَوُاْ النَّاسَ وَاخْشَوْنِ...﴾[272]

"Therefore fear not men but fear Me (O Jews)."

Allah(سبحانه وتعلى) says:

---

[270] Al-Anfal: 64
[271] Ali 'Imran: 175
[272] Al-Ma'idah: 44

﴿...فَإِيَّايَ فَارْهَبُونِ﴾[273]

"Then, fear Me (Allah) much."

In this verse, fear is singled out for Allah(سبحانه وتعلى) just as worship is singled out for Him in the following verse, Allah(سبحانه وتعلى) says:

﴿...فَإِيَّايَ فَاعْبُدُونِ﴾[274]

"Therefore worship Me (Alone)."

Piety: seeking Piety through the worship of Allah(سبحانه وتعلى) and His closeness, Allah(سبحانه وتعلى) says:

﴿وَإِيَّايَ فَاتَّقُونِ...﴾[275]

"And fear Me and Me Alone."

Allah(سبحانه وتعلى) says:

﴿...أَفَغَيْرَ اللَّهِ تَتَّقُونَ﴾[276]

"Will you then fear any other than Allah?"

Allah(سبحانه وتعلى) says:

﴿يَا أَيُّهَا الَّذِينَ آمَنُوا اتَّقُوا اللَّهَ وَقُولُوا قَوْلا سَدِيدًا * يُصْلِحْ لَكُمْ أَعْمَالَكُمْ وَيَغْفِرْ لَكُمْ ذُنُوبَكُمْ وَمَن يُطِعْ اللَّهَ وَرَسُولَهُ فَقَدْ فَازَ فَوْزًا عَظِيمًا﴾[277]

"O you who believe! Keep your duty to Allah and fear Him, and speak (always) the truth. He will direct you to do righteous deeds and will forgive your sins. And whosoever obeys Allah and His Messenger, he

[273] An-Nahl: 51
[274] Al-'Ankaboot: 56
[275] Al-Baqarah: 41
[276] An-Nahl: 52
[277] Al-Ahzab: 70-71

has indeed achieved a great achievement (i.e. he will be saved from the Hell-fire and made to enter Paradise)."

Tawheed al-Asma was-Sifat

Tawheed al-Asma was-Sifat (Oneness of the Names and Attributes of Allah(سبحانه وتعلى)): It is to single out Allah(سبحانه وتعلى) in His Names and Attributes by affirming for Allah(سبحانه وتعلى) what He has ascribed for Himself, whether in His book or through His Prophet ﷺ. [An affirmation is] without any alteration [changing its meaning] or suspension, or imagination [imagining any form or structure for Him] or resemblance [likening Him to any of His creation].

It is not allowed for anybody to nullify any of His Names or Attributes, which have been affirmed by Him. Allah(سبحانه وتعلى) says:

﴿وَلِلَّهِ الأَسْمَاء الْحُسْنَى فَادْعُوهُ بِهَا وَذَرُواْ الَّذِينَ يُلْحِدُونَ فِي أَسْمَآئِهِ سَيُجْزَوْنَ مَا كَانُواْ يَعْمَلُونَ﴾[278]

"And (all) the Most Beautiful Names belong to Allah, so call on Him by them, and leave the company of those who belie or deny (or utter impious speech against) His Names. They will be requited for what they used to do."

Because it leads to alteration or corruption of the texts, in addition to describing Allah(سبحانه وتعلى) with deficiencies and shortcomings.

It is also not allowed for anybody to name Allah(سبحانه وتعلى) or describe Him with anything, which is not introduced in the Book or in

[278] Al-A'raf: 180

the Prophetic narration. This is because it is like saying something about Allah(سبحانه وتعلى) without knowledge. Allah(سبحانه وتعلى) says:

﴿قُلْ إِنَّمَا حَرَّمَ رَبِّيَ الْفَوَاحِشَ مَا ظَهَرَ مِنْهَا وَمَا بَطَنَ وَالإِثْمَ وَالْبَغْيَ بِغَيْرِ الْحَقِّ وَأَن تُشْرِكُواْ بِاللَّهِ مَا لَمْ يُنَزِّلْ بِهِ سُلْطَانًا وَأَن تَقُولُواْ عَلَى اللَّهِ مَا لاَ تَعْلَمُونَ﴾[279]

"Say (O Muhammad): '(But) the things that my Lord has indeed forbidden are Al-Fawahish (great evil sins, every kind of unlawful sexual intercourse, etc.) whether committed openly or secretly, sins (of all kinds), unrighteous oppression, joining partners (in worship) with Allah for which He has given no authority, and saying things about Allah of which you have no knowledge.'"

Allah(سبحانه وتعلى) says:

﴿وَلاَ تَقْفُ مَا لَيْسَ لَكَ بِهِ عِلْمٌ إِنَّ السَّمْعَ وَالْبَصَرَ وَالْفُؤَادَ كُلُّ أُوْلَئِكَ كَانَ عَنْهُ مَسْؤُولاً﴾[280]

"And follow not (O man i.e., say not, or do not or witness not, etc.) that of which you have no knowledge (e.g. one's saying: 'I have seen,' while in fact he has not seen, or 'I have heard,' while he has not heard). Verily! The hearing, and the sight, and the heart, of each of those you will be questioned (by Allah)."

Likewise, it is not allowed to affirm Names or Attributes of Allah(سبحانه وتعلى) by likening Him to any of His creation. As Allah(سبحانه وتعلى) says:

﴿لَيْسَ كَمِثْلِهِ شَيْءٌ وَهُوَ السَّمِيعُ الْبَصِيرُ﴾[281]

"There is nothing like unto Him, and He is the All-Hearer, the All-Seer."

Allah(سبحانه وتعلى) says:

[279] Al-A'raf: 33
[280] Al-Isra': 36
[281] Ash-Shurah: 11

﴿فَلاَ تَضْرِبُواْ لِلَّهِ الأَمْثَالَ إِنَّ اللّهَ يَعْلَمُ وَأَنتُمْ لاَ تَعْلَمُونَ﴾[282]

"So put not forward similitudes for Allah (as there is nothing similar to Him, nor He resembles anything). Truly! Allah knows and you know not."

Because it leads to shirk, which necessitates the alteration or falsification of the texts, as well as the degradation of Allah(سبحانه وتعلى) by resembling Him to the imperfect creation.

It is not allowed to affirm any Name or Attribute of Allah(سبحانه وتعلى) while imagining it with any form or measure, because it is like saying something about Allah(سبحانه وتعلى) without knowledge. It leads to disorder and confusion about Allah(سبحانه وتعلى)'s Attributes because everybody will imagine a certain form or way different from the imagination of others. It is also considered as an attempt to perceive something which is beyond the human reason. So whatever shape or form imagines for Allah(سبحانه وتعلى), He is Greater and above all else.

There have been many contentions about this type of Tawheed, so the people have divided into six groups base on the texts.

The First Group: Those who interpret the verse according to its literal meaning, which is befitting with Allah(سبحانه وتعلى)'s majesty; without any alteration, suspension, imagination or resemblance. Those are the salaf, and this is the right opinion supported by the Qur'an, Sunnah, intellect, and consensus of the scholars, which has been previously established by textual and logical evidence.

The Second Group: Those who interpret according to its literal meaning, but they resemble it to the characteristics of the creation. Those people similitude Allah(سبحانه وتعلى) with His creation. Their

[282] An-Nahl: 74

methodology is invalidated by the Qur'an, Sunnah, and intellect and by the disproval of the Salaf.

The Third Group: Those who interpret the text contrary to its literal meaning, and they specify several meanings from their intellect, in doing so, they misinterpret the texts. Those people suspend the literal meaning. Some of them exceedingly suspend, like Jahmiyah and Mu'tazilah, while some others suspend but not to that extent, like Asha'irah.

The Fourth Group: Those who say: Allah(سبحانه وتعلى) knows best about what He intends with these Attributes. In doing so, they refer the knowledge of the meaning of the Attributes to Him only. These are the ignorant that pass over [the interpretation]. Few amongst them disagree with the previous statement saying: that Allah(سبحانه وتعلى) knows best what He intends; however, there is no evidence to indicate the affirmation of His external attributes.

The Fifth Group: Those who say that it is possible that these texts are meant to affirm the Attributes for Allah(سبحانه وتعلى), which are befitting with His Majesty, but they do not comply with it. Among them are many of the jurists and others.

The Sixth Group: Those who avoid the interpretation of these texts altogether. They only read these verses and do not want to think or talk about it.[283]

All of these groups, except the first one, have deviated from the right path, as it has been previously clarified in more than one occasion.

[283] These groups were mentioned in *Al-Fatwa al-Hamawiyah*, p. (156-162).

A false understanding of the majority of the philosophers regarding the categories of Tawheed

From the previous discussion of types of Tawheed, the errors of the majority of the philosophers become clear regarding the conventional classification of Tawheed, whereupon they have divided it into three types:

The First: Allah(سبحانه وتعلى) is One in His Being; He has neither a partner nor a part.

The Second: He is One in His Attributes and nothing is similar to Him.

The Third: He is One in His actions; without any association.

Explanation of Their Errors:

- ✓ They do not include Tawheed al-Uluhiyah; which is acknowledging the Oneness of the Worship of Allah(سبحانه وتعالى), without any partners; thus, He should be singled out in worship. Allah(سبحانه وتعلى) has created Jinn and mankind only to fulfill this type of Tawheed.

Allah(سبحانه وتعلى) says:

﴿وَمَا خَلَقْتُ الْجِنَّ وَالإِنسَ إِلاَّ لِيَعْبُدُونِ﴾[284]

"And I (Allah) created not the jinn and mankind except that they should worship Me (Alone)."

For this reason, Allah(سبحانه وتعلى) has sent down the messengers and the books. Allah(سبحانه وتعلى) says:

[284] Adh-Dhariyat-56.

﴿وَمَا أَرْسَلْنَا مِن قَبْلِكَ مِن رَّسُولٍ إِلاَّ نُوحِي إِلَيْهِ أَنَّهُ لا إِلَهَ إِلاَّ أَنَا فَاعْبُدُونِ﴾[285]

"And We did not send any Messenger before you but We revealed to Him (saying): None has the right to be worshiped but I (Allah), so worship Me (Alone and none else)."

Allah(سبحانه وتعلى) says:

﴿وَلَقَدْ بَعَثْنَا فِي كُلِّ أُمَّةٍ رَّسُولاً أَنِ اعْبُدُواْ اللَّهَ وَاجْتَنِبُواْ الطَّاغُوتَ...﴾[286]

"And verily, We have sent among every Ummah (community, nation) a Messenger (proclaiming): 'Worship Allah (Alone), and avoid (or keep away from) Taghut (all false deities, etc. i.e. do not worship Taghut besides Allah).'"

The messengers used to call people to this message. Allah(سبحانه وتعلى) says:

﴿...أَنِ اعْبُدُوا اللَّهَ مَا لَكُم مِّنْ إِلَهٍ غَيْرُهُ...﴾[287]

"Worship Allah! You have no other Ilah (God) but Him."

Meaning, there is no true God except Allah(سبحانه وتعلى); all other deities are false, as Allah(سبحانه وتعلى) says:

﴿ذَلِكَ بِأَنَّ اللَّهَ هُوَ الْحَقُّ وَأَنَّ مَا يَدْعُونَ مِن دُونِهِ الْبَاطِلُ وَأَنَّ اللَّهَ هُوَ الْعَلِيُّ الْكَبِيرُ﴾[288]

"That is because Allah, He is the Truth, and that which they invoke besides Him is Al-Batil (falsehood, Satan and all other false deities), and that Allah, He is the Most High, the Most Great."

---

[285] Al-Anbiya': 25
[286] An-Nahl: 36
[287] Al-Mu'mineen: 32
[288] Luqman: 30

And for this purpose, the debates and the battles have emerged between the messengers and their people, who have rejected their message.

As Allah(سبحانه وتعلى) says about the people of Nuh:

﴿قَالُواْ يَا نُوحُ قَدْ جَادَلْتَنَا فَأَكْثَرْتَ جِدَالَنَا فَأْتِنَا بِمَا تَعِدُنَا إِن كُنتَ مِنَ الصَّادِقِينَ﴾[289]

"They said: 'O Nuh (Noah)! You have disputed with us and much have you prolonged the dispute with us, now bring upon us what you threaten us with if you are of the truthful."

Allah(سبحانه وتعلى) says about the people of Hud:

﴿قَالُواْ يَا هُودُ مَا جِئْتَنَا بِبَيِّنَةٍ وَمَا نَحْنُ بِتَارِكِي آلِهَتِنَا عَن قَوْلِكَ وَمَا نَحْنُ لَكَ بِمُؤْمِنِينَ * إِن نَّقُولُ إِلاَّ اعْتَرَاكَ بَعْضُ آلِهَتِنَا بِسُوءٍ قَالَ إِنِّي أُشْهِدُ اللّهَ وَاشْهَدُواْ أَنِّي بَرِيءٌ مِّمَّا تُشْرِكُونَ *مِن دُونِهِ فَكِيدُونِي جَمِيعًا ثُمَّ لاَ تُنظِرُونِ﴾[290]

"They said: 'O Hud! No evidence have you brought us, and we shall not leave our gods for your (mere) saying! And we are not believers in you. All that we say is that some of our gods (false deities) have seized you with evil (madness).' He said: 'I call Allah to witness and bear you witness that I am free from that which you ascribe as partners in worship, - With Him (Allah). So plot against me, all of you, and give me no respite.'"

Allah(سبحانه وتعلى) says about Ibrahim and his people:

﴿قَالَ أَفَتَعْبُدُونَ مِن دُونِ اللَّهِ مَا لا يَنفَعُكُمْ شَيْئًا وَلا يَضُرُّكُمْ *أُفٍّ لَّكُمْ وَلِمَا تَعْبُدُونَ مِن دُونِ اللَّهِ أَفَلا تَعْقِلُونَ * قَالُوا حَرِّقُوهُ وَانصُرُوا آلِهَتَكُمْ إِن كُنتُمْ فَاعِلِينَ * قُلْنَا يَا نَارُ كُونِي بَرْدًا وَسَلامًا عَلَى إِبْرَاهِيمَ﴾[291]

[289] Hud: 32
[290] Ibid: 53-55
[291] Al-Anbiya': 66-69

"[Ibrahim (Abraham)] said: 'Do you then worship besides Allah, things that can neither profit you, nor harm you? Fie upon you, and upon that which you worship besides Allah! Have you then no sense?' They said: 'Burn him and help your aaliha (gods), if you will be doing.' We (Allah) said: 'O fire! Be you coolness and safety for Ibrahim (Abraham)!'

Allah(سبحانه وتعلى) says about the disbelievers in Mohammad ﷺ:

﴿وَإِذَا رَآكَ الَّذِينَ كَفَرُوا إِن يَتَّخِذُونَكَ إِلاَّ هُزُوًا أَهَذَا الَّذِي يَذْكُرُ آلِهَتَكُمْ...﴾[292]

"And when those who disbelieve (in the Oneness of Allah) see you (O Muhammad), they take you not except for mockery (saying): 'Is this the one who talks (badly) about your gods?'"

Allah(سبحانه وتعلى) says:

﴿وَعَجِبُوا أَن جَاءَهُم مُّنذِرٌ مِّنْهُمْ وَقَالَ الْكَافِرُونَ هَذَا سَاحِرٌ كَذَّابٌ * أَجَعَلَ الآلِهَةَ إِلَهًا وَاحِدًا إِنَّ هَذَا لَشَيْءٌ عُجَابٌ * وَانطَلَقَ الْمَلأُ مِنْهُمْ أَنِ امْشُوا وَاصْبِرُوا عَلَى آلِهَتِكُمْ إِنَّ هَذَا لَشَيْءٌ يُرَادُ﴾[293]

"And they (Arab pagans) wonder that a warner (Prophet Muhammad) has come to them from among themselves! And the disbelievers say: 'This (Prophet Muhammad) is a sorcerer, a liar. Has he made the aliha (gods) (all) into One Ilah (God - Allah)? Verily, this is a curious thing!' And the leaders among them went about (saying): 'Go on, and remain constant to your gods! Verily, This is a thing designed (against you)!'"

Allah(سبحانه وتعلى) says about his enemies:

﴿إِن يَثْقَفُوكُمْ يَكُونُوا لَكُمْ أَعْدَاء وَيَبْسُطُوا إِلَيْكُمْ أَيْدِيَهُمْ وَأَلْسِنَتَهُم بِالسُّوءِ وَوَدُّوا لَوْ تَكْفُرُونَ﴾[294]

---

[292] Ibid: 36
[293] Sad: 4-6
[294] Al-Mumtahinah: 2

"Should they gain the upper hand over you, they would behave to you as enemies, and stretch forth their hands and their tongues against you with evil, and they desire that you should disbelieve."

Although Tawheed al-Uluhiyah bears such a significant role, the majority of the philosophers neglect it. This negligence is one of their errors in their conventional classification of Tawheed.

- ✓ Their statement: "Allah(سبحانه وتعلى) is One in His Being; He has neither a partner nor a part," is general and needs clarification:

If they mean by it that, Allah(سبحانه وتعلى) cannot be divided into pieces or His being is not a combination of pieces, it is right. Because He is the One, the Self-Sufficient Master. He begets not, nor is He begotten. There is none co-equal or comparable unto Him.

But if they mean by it, that the negation of His Attributes, which He has affirmed for Himself, such as His Highness, rising on 'Arsh, His Face, Hands and so on – and this is what they mean – then, it is invalid. Indeed, Allah(سبحانه وتعلى) has affirmed attributes of perfection such as these as well as the others, which are befitting with His Majesty. The fulfillment of Tawheed here is to affirm these Attributes for Allah(سبحانه وتعلى) in a manner that is befitting with His Majesty, without resemblance; not by alteration or suspension.

- ✓ Their statement: "He is One in His Attributes and nothing is similar to Him," is general and needs clarification:

If they mean by it, affirming Attributes of Allah(سبحانه وتعلى), in a way that is befitting with His Majesty, without resembling Him to anything about something specific and special to Him, then it is true and it is the opinion of the Salaf. However, most of the philosophers do not intend this [meaning].

If they mean by it, that negating [absolute] resemblance between the creation and Allah(سبحانه وتعلى) from every aspect, then this is indeed senseless. It is like someone saying: The heaven is above us and the earth is below us. Indeed, the resemblance of the Creator to the creation in every aspect is clearly negated; rather it is prohibited by virtue of reason, textual evidence, and the consensus of every rational person. That is why no nation has ever claimed that someone resembles Allah(سبحانه وتعلى) in every aspect; if they do claim any resemblance, then the most that occur is resembling Him in a few aspects.

And if they mean by it, that negating [general] resemblance between Allah(سبحانه وتعلى) and the creation, so as to negate any common characteristics between them even while distinguishing between them in what is unique for each, – and this is what they mean – then, it is invalid. It is known by virtue of reason that there are no two existing beings except that they share some common characteristics; yet, they are different from each other in some other special characteristics. Some corresponding common characteristics are their existence, being, self-establishment, and so on. Negating this share is an absolute suspension.

This opinion does not exclude the negation of the affirmed Attributes of perfection; since they may claim that affirming these will necessitate resemblance. It has been previously mentioned that the people of suspension [تعطيل] amongst Al-Jahmiyah, Al-Mu'tazilah and others include the negation of the Attributes in their conventional meaning of Tawheed. They say that whoever affirms the Attributes of Knowledge, Power and the like, he will be considered as Mushabbih [i.e. one who resembles Allah(سبحانه وتعلى) to creation] rather than a monotheist. Moreover, the extreme philosophers, like Al-Qarâmitah, further include in it [the conventional meaning of tawheed] the negation of the Names; thus, they say that whoever claims that Allah(سبحانه وتعلى) is Knowledgeable, Powerful and so on, he is considered as Mushabbih, not a monotheist. The most extreme of the extremists further add that

Allah(سبحانه وتعلى) should not be described by anything that includes affirmation or negation; therefore, whoever negates or affirms any attribute for Allah(سبحانه وتعلى), then he is considered as Mushabbih, not a monotheist.

The refutation of their arguments has been discussed at the beginning of this book, and all praise be to Allah(سبحانه وتعلى).

- ✓ Their statement: "Allah(سبحانه وتعلى) is One in His action without association." This type of Tawheed is the most well-known amongst them. They mean by this that the Creator of the world is One, assuming that this is the genuine Tawheed and that this is the meaning of (La ilaaha illaa Allah). In doing so, they alter it to mean, "Nobody is capable to innovate but Allah(سبحانه وتعلى)."

This concept is wrong from two angles:

- o Their statement has been acknowledged earlier by Mushrikeen, whom the Prophet ﷺ has fought against. They have not associated anybody with Allah(سبحانه وتعلى) in His actions.

As Allah(سبحانه وتعلى) says:

﴿وَلَئِن سَأَلْتَهُم مَّنْ خَلَقَ السَّمَاوَاتِ وَالأَرْضَ وَسَخَّرَ الشَّمْسَ وَالْقَمَرَ لَيَقُولُنَّ اللَّهُ فَأَنَّى يُؤْفَكُونَ﴾[295]

"If you were to ask them: 'Who has created the heavens and the earth and subjected the sun and the moon?' They will surely reply: 'Allah'. How then are they deviating (as polytheists and disbelievers)?"

﴿وَلَئِن سَأَلْتَهُم مَّنْ خَلَقَهُمْ لَيَقُولُنَّ اللَّهُ﴾[296]

"And if you ask them who created them, they will surely say: 'Allah'.

[295] Al-'Ankabut: 61.
[296] Zukhruf: 87.

Although they acknowledge it, they are still Mushrikun and not monotheists, as established by the Qur'an, Sunnah, and Ijmaa as well. This is due to their negligence of Tawheed al-Uluhiyah. They say:

﴿أَجَعَلَ الآلِهَةَ إِلَهًا وَاحِدًا إِنَّ هَذَا لَشَيْءٌ عُجَابٌ﴾[297]

"Has he made the aliha (gods) (all) into One Ilah (God - Allah). Verily, this is a curious thing!"

That is why the Prophet ﷺ has fought against them, legalized their blood, wealth and has allowed taking their children and wives as slaves.

- Their interpretation of (La ilâha illâ Allâh) which has been mentioned; that nobody is capable to innovate but Allah(سبحانه وتعلى); necessitates that whosoever recognizes that only Allah(سبحانه وتعلى) alone is capable to innovate, then he has testified that La ilâha illâ Allâh, and his blood and wealth are safeguarded.

According to the above discussion, it is clear that their interpretation of (La ilaaha illaa Allah) is invalid and not in line with the Muslims beliefs. The accurate interpretation of (La ilaaha illaa Allah) is: "There is no god worthy of being worshiped except Allah", this is the meaning known to Muslims and Mushrikun as well. The following verse proves the reality of our evidence:

Allah(سبحانه وتعلى) says:

﴿إِنَّهُمْ كَانُوا إِذَا قِيلَ لَهُمْ لا إِلَهَ إِلاَّ اللهُ يَسْتَكْبِرُونَ * وَيَقُولُونَ أَئِنَّا لَتَارِكُوا آلِهَتِنَا لِشَاعِرٍ مَّجْنُونٍ﴾[298]

"Truly, when it was said to them: La ilaha ill- Allah '(none has the right to be worshipped but Allah),' they puffed themselves up with pride (i.e.

[297] Sad: 5.
[298] As-Saaffaat:35-36.

denied it). And (they) said: 'Are we going to abandon our aliha (gods) for the sake of a mad poet?"'

They are not arrogant to acknowledge with their hearts as well as tongues that Allah(سبحانه وتعلى) is the only Creator, neither do they claim that their gods create something. Thus, it becomes clear that the Mushrikun are more knowledgeable and smarter about Tawheed than those philosophers are. The most that these philosophers acknowledge from Tawheed is Tawheed ar-Rububiyah; which neither frees man from shirk nor does it safeguard his wealth and blood and nor will he be safe from abiding eternally in the Hell-fire.

This interpretation has been adopted by some Sufi groups who belong to al-Ma'rifah, at-Tahqeeq, and al-Tawheed. According to them, the epitome of Tawheed is to testify that Allah(سبحانه وتعلى) is the Lord, Owner and the Creator of everything. This is [attained] especially when the Aaarif delves within his Source of existence away from existence, within his Witness away from witnesses, within the One who knows him away from those he knows, and once he enters the domain of Tawheed ar-Rububiyah, whereupon the one who has never existed perishes and the one who exists remains.

It is known that this intent of Tawheed has been adopted by the Mushrikeen. Nevertheless, it does not make one, a Muslim, neither does it make him from the close friends of Allah(سبحانه وتعلى) or superior over His creation.

Fana' (Perish) and its categories

Linguistic Meaning: Fana' means to perish, Allah(سبحانه وتعلى) says:

﴿كُلُّ مَنْ عَلَيْهَا فَانٍ * وَيَبْقَى وَجْهُ رَبِّكَ ذُو الْجَلَالِ وَالإِكْرَامِ﴾[299]

"Whatsoever is on the earth will perish. And the Face of your Lord full of Majesty and Honor will remain forever."

Conventional Meaning: Fana' has three categories:

The First Category (Sacred Legislative Definition)

[ديني شرعي]: Fana' means the act of eliminating any desire for others, meaning, eliminating desires for anything other than Allah(سبحانه وتعلى).

Thus, one eliminates polytheism to attain sincerity for Allah(سبحانه وتعالى); eliminates innovation to fulfill His legislation; eliminates His disobedience to fulfill His obedience; eliminates dependence on others to fulfill reliance on Allah(سبحانه وتعلى); and eliminates oneself's wishes to enact the wish of his Lord and the similar actions that busy one from seeking the pleasure of Allah(سبحانه وتعلى).

Its reality is for the slave to busy himself with whatever brings him closer to Allah(سبحانه وتعلى) over anything that would otherwise distance him from Allah(سبحانه وتعلى). However, attaching with these things can be called Fana' in their conventional meaning.

This is the legislative [commended] Fana' that the Prophets have come with, and for which the books have been revealed, and through which the religion becomes established, and the success in this world and the next is attained.

Allah(سبحانه وتعلى) says:

﴿وَمَنْ أَرَادَ الآخِرَةَ وَسَعَى لَهَا سَعْيَهَا وَهُوَ مُؤْمِنٌ فَأُولَئِكَ كَانَ سَعْيُهُم مَّشْكُورًا﴾[300]

---

[299] Al-Rahman: 26-27.
[300] Al-Isra': 19

"And whoever desires the Hereafter and strives for it, with the necessary effort due for it (i.e. do righteous deeds of Allah's Obedience) while he is a believer (in the Oneness of Allah, Islamic Monotheism), then such are the ones whose striving shall be appreciated, thanked and rewarded (by Allah)."

Allah(سبحانه وتعلى) says:

﴿مَنْ عَمِلَ صَالِحًا مِّن ذَكَرٍ أَوْ أُنثَى وَهُوَ مُؤْمِنٌ فَلَنُحْيِيَنَّهُ حَيَاةً طَيِّبَةً وَلَنَجْزِيَنَّهُمْ أَجْرَهُم بِأَحْسَنِ مَا كَانُواْ يَعْمَلُونَ﴾[301]

"Whoever works righteousness, whether male or female, while he (or she) is a true believer (of Islamic Monotheism) verily, to him We will give a good life (in this world with respect, contentment and lawful provision), and We shall pay them certainly a reward in proportion to the best of what they used to do (i.e. Paradise in the Hereafter)."

Allah(سبحانه وتعلى) says:

﴿وَالَّذِينَ صَبَرُواْ ابْتِغَاء وَجْهِ رَبِّهِمْ وَأَقَامُواْ الصَّلاَةَ وَأَنفَقُواْ مِمَّا رَزَقْنَاهُمْ سِرًّا وَعَلاَنِيَةً وَيَدْرَؤُونَ بِالْحَسَنَةِ السَّيِّئَةَ أُوْلَئِكَ لَهُمْ عُقْبَى الدَّارِ﴾[302]

"And those who remain patient, seeking their Lord's Countenance, perform As-Salat (Iqamat-as-Salat), and spend out of that which We have bestowed on them, secretly and openly, and defend evil with good, for such there is a good end."

Allah(سبحانه وتعلى) says:

﴿يَا أَيُّهَا الَّذِينَ آمَنُوا لا تُلْهِكُمْ أَمْوَالُكُمْ وَلا أَوْلادُكُمْ عَن ذِكْرِ اللَّهِ وَمَن يَفْعَلْ ذَلِكَ فَأُوْلَئِكَ هُمُ الْخَاسِرُونَ﴾[303]

---

[301] An-Nahl: 97
[302] Al-RaÑd: 22
[303] Al-Munafiqoon: 9

"O you who believe! Let not your properties or your children divert you from the remembrance of Allah. And whosoever does that, then they are the losers."

This is the real taste of Imaan, which nothing can compare to. It is mentioned in Sahihain, on the authority of Anas bin Maalik ﷺ that the Prophet says: "Whoever possesses the following three qualities will have the sweetness (delight) of faith: the one to whom Allah and His messenger become dearer than anything else, who loves a person only for Allah's sake, and who hates to revert to atheism (disbelief) as he hates to be thrown into the fire."[304]

And Sahih Muslim reports on the authority of 'Abbâs bin 'Abdul Muttalib ﷺ that he has heard the Prophet ﷺ says: "He relished the favor of faith (Eemân) who become pleased with Allah as Lord, with al-Islam as the code of life, and with Mohammad as the Messenger of Allah".[305]

The Second Category (Innovated Mystical Meaning) [صوفي بدعي]: Fana' means the act of transcending any awareness of others, meaning to transcend any awareness of other than Allah(سبحانه وتعلى). This results from the attachment of one's heart to Allah(سبحانه وتعلى); thus, the weakness to bear this attachment and its demands make the heart unaware of anything except Allah(سبحانه وتعلى). Thus, he delves within his unconsciousness at which point he transcends any awareness for anything other than Him. He transcends worship for Allah(سبحانه وتعلى) and transcends Dhikr for the One remembered until he is no longer aware whether he is in the act of worship and Dhikr or not because he is oblivious to all that due to the overwhelming power of this attachment.

---

[304] Al-Bukhari, Book: Eemân, Chapter: The sweetness of Eemân, No. (16); Muslim, Book: Eemân, Chapter: The sweetness of Eemân, No. (42,43).

[305] Muslim, Book of Faith, Chapter: He has tasted Eemân who was pleased with Allah as Lord… No. (34).

This kind of Fana' is admired by some Sufi leaders; however, this opinion is not accepted because of the following reasons:

- It is indicative of the weakness of the person's heart because he is not able to integrate between the presence of Allah(سبحانه وتعالى) and worship Him as well as between Allah(سبحانه وتعلى) and His commands. He thinks that being busy with worship and commands makes him away from Allah(سبحانه وتعلى).
- This kind of thinking makes the person similar to mad or drunken people, to the extent that strange and nonsensical acts and statements may come out of him, which are clearly against the laws of Allah(سبحانه وتعلى) – an error that is obvious both to him and others. For example, some people have said in such a situation, "Glory be to me, glory be to me… I am Allah(سبحانه وتعلى). What is inside this Jubbah [loose outer garment] is nothing but Allah(سبحانه وتعلى). I shall put my tent on the Hell-fire," and similar odd, preposterous statements.
- This type of Fana' [transcendence] has never been practiced by the sincere righteous slaves of Allah(سبحانه وتعلى). It has never been practiced by the messengers, or the prophets, or the righteous, or the martyrs. Indeed, during the night of Mi'raj, the Prophet ﷺ witnessed some signs of Allah(سبحانه وتعلى)'s supremacy, which has never happened to anyone. Yet, in that situation, he was in a state of full consciousness, physically and internally. Allah(سبحانه وتعلى) says about his physical strength:

﴿مَا زَاغَ الْبَصَرُ وَمَا طَغَى﴾[306]

"The sight (of Prophet Muhammad) turned not aside (right or left), nor it transgressed beyond (the) limit (ordained for it)."

---

[306] An-Najm: 17

Allah(سبحانه وتعلى) says about his internal strength:

﴿مَا كَذَبَ الْفُؤَادُ مَا رَأَى﴾[307]

"The (Prophet's) heart lied not (in seeing) what he (Muhammad ﷺ) saw."

Neither the rightly guided caliphs, who are the leaders of the people and the best generation after the prophets – Abu Bakar, 'Umar, 'Uthmân and 'Ali ﷺ – nor the rest of the companions, who occupy esteemed positions, have ever been involved in this type of transcendence.

Indeed, it was first introduced during the era of the tâbi'een [of the third generation]. Some of these devotees used to shout, while some others used to be fall unconscious to the extent that some of them died during Fana'. It was commonly known amongst some Sufi leaders.

Whoever considers this to be the epitome of devotion, [and that this is the way of the righteous people], then he is clearly misguided. And whoever thinks it is of the necessities in coming closer to Allah(سبحانه وتعالى), then he has erred.

Its reality is that it is of the symptoms that occur to some of the mystical people, due to the overwhelming power of the experience on their hearts and their weakness in overcoming it as well as in integrating between worship and the One worshipped, and so on.

The Third Category (Faithless Atheistic Meaning)

[الحادي كفري]: Fana' means the act of dissociating from the existence of others, meaning the existence of other than Allah(سبحانه وتعلى). They think that the creator himself is the creature and that the created being itself is the sustainer. According to them, there is no difference between

[307] Ibid: 11

the Lord and the slave, the creator and the creature, the worshiper and One worshiped and the Commander and commanded; all these things are the same being.

This type of Fana' is the methodology of the atheists, those who believe in the unity of existence [وحدة الوجود], like ibn 'Arabi, Tilmisani, ibn Sab'een, al-Qawnawi, and so on. They are greater disbelievers than the Christians, from two perspectives:

◊ Those people consider the Lord and the Creator Himself as sustained and created, while the Christians believe about the union of the Lord with His chosen slave after they have been separated.
◊ Those people generalize the unity of the Lord with everything, even within dogs, pigs, rubbish and so on; however, those Christians restrict this unity with someone special, whom they respect, like Jesus.[308]

A simple consideration of this claim is enough to counter it since it necessitates that the Lord and the slave are one, the eater and the thing eaten are one, the married couples are one, the suspect and the judge are one, and the witness and witnessed against are one. This is the epitome of ignorance and misguidance.

The Shaykh, may Allah(سبحانه وتعلى) have mercy on him, says: He mentions about one of them that he cohabits his son and claims that he [his son] is Allah(سبحانه وتعلى), the Lord of the worlds. May Allah(سبحانه وتعلى) curse the group of people who consider those they cohabit as their Lords!

Ibn al-Qayyim, may Allah(سبحانه وتعلى) have mercy on him, speaks about this group in his poem [An-Nooniyyah]:

[308] See: Majmoo' al-Fatâwâ by Ibn al-Qâsim (2/172).

> The sect deemed Him not far above Humans, demon, animals, and trees,
>
> Yet, they made Him the food, the cloth, the perceived and what is heard by the ears,
>
> They also said it is He who is copulated and slaughtered, even said to be the adulterer.

He continues until he says:

> This is the deity they worship so, say: Glory be to you Allah (سبحنه وتعلى), the Glorified!
>
> Oh, Nation, whose Deity is the copulated, you claim suprasternal notch to be Allah!! You falsified.
>
> Oh, Nation! The absolute apostasy equals the slight apostasy of yours.

True Perfection of Islam

One's Islam is not complete unless it is free from everything else [other than Islam]. Allah(سبحانه وتعلى) says about His friend Ibrahim ﷺ:

﴿وَإِذْ قَالَ إِبْرَاهِيمُ لِأَبِيهِ وَقَوْمِهِ إِنَّنِي بَرَاءٌ مِّمَّا تَعْبُدُونَ * إِلاَّ الَّذِي فَطَرَنِي فَإِنَّهُ سَيَهْدِينِ * وَجَعَلَهَا كَلِمَةً بَاقِيَةً فِي عَقِبِهِ لَعَلَّهُمْ يَرْجِعُونَ﴾[309]*

"And (remember) when Ibrahim (Abraham) said to his father and his people: 'Verily, I am innocent of what you worship, Except Him (i.e. I worship none but Allah Alone) Who did create me, and verily, He will

[309] Az-Zukhruf: 26-28.

guide me.' And he made it [i.e. La ilaha ill-Allah (none has the right to be worshipped but Allah Alone)] a Word lasting among his offspring (True Monotheism), that they may turn back (i.e. to repent to Allah or receive admonition)."

Allah(سبحانه وتعلى) also describes Ibrahim as the best model for us to follow; He says:

﴿قَدْ كَانَتْ لَكُمْ أُسْوَةٌ حَسَنَةٌ فِي إِبْرَاهِيمَ وَالَّذِينَ مَعَهُ إِذْ قَالُوا لِقَوْمِهِمْ إِنَّا بُرَاء مِنكُمْ وَمِمَّا تَعْبُدُونَ مِن دُونِ اللَّهِ كَفَرْنَا بِكُمْ وَبَدَا بَيْنَنَا وَبَيْنَكُمُ الْعَدَاوَةُ وَالْبَغْضَاء أَبَدًا حَتَّى تُؤْمِنُوا بِاللَّهِ وَحْدَهُ﴾310

"Indeed there has been an excellent example for you in Ibrahim (Abraham) and those with him, when they said to their people: 'Verily, we are free from you and whatever you worship besides Allah, we have rejected you, and there has started between us and you, hostility and hatred forever, until you believe in Allah Alone.'"

Allah(سبحانه وتعلى) says:

﴿يَا أَيُّهَا الَّذِينَ آمَنُوا لا تَتَّخِذُوا عَدُوِّي وَعَدُوَّكُمْ أَوْلِيَاء تُلْقُونَ إِلَيْهِم بِالْمَوَدَّةِ وَقَدْ كَفَرُوا بِمَا جَاءَكُم مِّنَ الْحَقِّ﴾[311]

"O you who believe! Take not My enemies and your enemies (i.e. disbelievers and polytheists, etc.) as friends, showing affection towards them, while they have disbelieved in what has come to you of the truth."

Allah(سبحانه وتعلى) says:

﴿يَا أَيُّهَا الَّذِينَ آمَنُواْ لاَ تَتَّخِذُواْ الْيَهُودَ وَالنَّصَارَى أَوْلِيَاء بَعْضُهُمْ أَوْلِيَاء بَعْضٍ وَمَن يَتَوَلَّهُم مِّنكُمْ فَتَرَى الَّذِينَ فِي قُلُوبِهِم مَّرَضٌ يُسَارِعُونَ فِيهِمْ * فَإِنَّهُ مِنْهُمْ إِنَّ اللّهَ لاَ يَهْدِي الْقَوْمَ الظَّالِمِينَ

[310] Al-Mumtahanah: 4.
[311] Ibid: 1

يَقُولُونَ نَخْشَى أَن تُصِيبَنَا دَائِرَةٌ فَعَسَى اللَّهُ أَن يَأْتِيَ بِالْفَتْحِ أَوْ أَمْرٍ مِّنْ عِندِهِ فَيُصْبِحُوا عَلَى مَا أَسَرُّوا فِي أَنفُسِهِمْ نَادِمِينَ﴾[312]

"O you who believe! Take not the Jews and the Christians as Auliya' (friends, protectors, helpers, etc.), they are but Auliya' to one another. And if any amongst you takes them as Auliya', then surely he is one of them. Verily, Allah guides not those people who are the Zalimun (polytheists and wrong-doers and unjust). And you see those in whose hearts there is a disease (of hypocrisy), they hurry to their friendship, saying: 'We fear lest some misfortune of a disaster may befall us.' Perhaps Allah may bring a victory or a decision according to His Will. Then they will become regretful for what they have been keeping as a secret in themselves."

Allah(سبحانه وتعلى) says:

﴿لا تَجِدُ قَوْمًا يُؤْمِنُونَ بِاللَّهِ وَالْيَوْمِ الآخِرِ يُوَادُّونَ مَنْ حَادَّ اللَّهَ وَرَسُولَهُ وَلَوْ كَانُوا آبَاءَهُمْ أَوْ أَبْنَاءَهُمْ أَوْ إِخْوَانَهُمْ أَوْ عَشِيرَتَهُمْ أُوْلَئِكَ كَتَبَ فِي قُلُوبِهِمُ الإِيمَانَ وَأَيَّدَهُم بِرُوحٍ مِّنْهُ وَيُدْخِلُهُمْ جَنَّاتٍ تَجْرِي مِن تَحْتِهَا الأَنْهَارُ خَالِدِينَ فِيهَا رَضِيَ اللَّهُ عَنْهُمْ وَرَضُوا عَنْهُ أُوْلَئِكَ حِزْبُ اللَّهِ أَلا إِنَّ حِزْبَ اللَّهِ هُمُ الْمُفْلِحُونَ﴾[313]

"You (O Muhammad) will not find any people who believe in Allah and the Last Day, making friendship with those who oppose Allah and His Messenger (Muhammad), even though they were their fathers, or their sons, or their brothers, or their kindred (people). For such He has written Faith in their hearts, and strengthened them with Ruh (proofs, light and true guidance) from Himself. And We will admit them to Gardens (Paradise) under which rivers flow, to dwell therein (forever). Allah is pleased with them, and they with Him. They are the Party of Allah. Verily, it is the Party of Allah that will be the successful."

The innocence of Islam [free of everything else] is of two types:

[312] Al-Mâ'idah: 52
[313] Al-Mujâdalah:22

I. Innocence From the Action
II. Innocence From the Doer

As for innocence from the action: It is to be innocent of every prohibited action, whether it is kufr or less than that. So the believer should be innocent of shirk, adultery, drinking of wine and so on; that he should neither be pleased with it nor approve of it or use it. Indeed, doing such things is opposing to Allah(سبحانه وتعلى) and His pleasure.

As for innocence from the doer: If someone's actions are blasphemous [kufr], then one must be innocent of him in every way possible, according to the aforementioned verses, because he is not deserving of friendship.

If his actions are less than kufr, then one must be innocent of him regarding the aspects related to kufr; yet, friendship should be kept regarding other aspects related to belief and good deeds. This is because wrongdoing does not negate absolute belief; indeed, one person can have some bad characteristics as well as good characteristics; likewise, he can have some characteristic of belief as well as the characteristic of disbelief.

Allah(سبحانه وتعلى) says:

﴿وَإِن طَائِفَتَانِ مِنَ الْمُؤْمِنِينَ اقْتَتَلُوا فَأَصْلِحُوا بَيْنَهُمَا فَإِن بَغَتْ إِحْدَاهُمَا عَلَى الْأُخْرَى فَقَاتِلُوا الَّتِي تَبْغِي حَتَّى تَفِيءَ إِلَى أَمْرِ اللَّهِ فَإِن فَاءَتْ فَأَصْلِحُوا بَيْنَهُمَا بِالْعَدْلِ وَأَقْسِطُوا إِنَّ اللَّهَ يُحِبُّ الْمُقْسِطِينَ * إِنَّمَا الْمُؤْمِنُونَ إِخْوَةٌ فَأَصْلِحُوا بَيْنَ أَخَوَيْكُمْ﴾[314]

"And if two parties or groups among the believers fall to fighting, then make peace between them both, but if one of them rebels against the other, then fight you (all) against the one that which rebels till it complies with the Command of Allah; then if it complies, then make reconciliation between them justly, and be equitable. Verily! Allah loves

[314] Al-Hujurat: 9-10

those who are equitable. The believers are nothing else than brothers (in Islamic religion). So make reconciliation between your brothers, and fear Allah, that you may receive mercy."

In these verses, Allah(سبحانه وتعلى) refers to the two fighting groups as brethren for the reconciling group, and describes them as believers even though fighting other believers is considered as kufr according to a prophetic narration.

The Prophet ﷺ says: "Abusing a Muslim is Fusooq [an evil doing] and combating him is kufr [disbelief]."[315]

This characteristic of kufr neither does it cancel the basis of Eemân nor does it anull the religious bond of brotherhood. There is no doubt, however, that the Islamic bond of brotherhood is based upon love and friendship, which is proportional to the degree of Eemân and steadfastness. This basic principle – that a person may have both characteristics of belief and disbelief – has been proven by the Qur'an, Sunnah as well as by the early Muslim scholars. Therefore, love and friendship will be proportional to the amount of Eemân he has; likewise, hatred and enmity will be proportional to the amount of kufr he has [brotherhood will increase according to the Eemân and it will decrease according to the kufr].

The believer is commanded to do righteous deeds and to avoid prohibited deeds (Evils)

The believer is commanded to enact the righteous deeds, avoid prohibited deeds, and to be patient with his fate.

[315] Al-Bukhari. The Book of Belief (Faith), Chapter: Regarding the believer's fear that his good deeds may be annulled (lost) without realizing.

Allah(سبحانه وتعلى) says:

﴿يَا أَيُّهَا الَّذِينَ آمَنُواْ اصْبِرُواْ وَصَابِرُواْ وَرَابِطُواْ وَاتَّقُواْ اللّهَ لَعَلَّكُمْ تُفْلِحُونَ﴾[316]

"O you who believe! Endure and be more patient (than your enemy), and guard your territory by stationing army units permanently at the places from where the enemy can attack you, and fear Allah, so that you may be successful."

And Allah(سبحانه وتعلى) says:

﴿...إِنَّهُ مَن يَتَّقِ وَيِصْبِرْ فَإِنَّ اللّهَ لاَ يُضِيعُ أَجْرَ الْمُحْسِنِينَ﴾[317]

"Verily, he who fears Allah with obedience to Him (by abstaining from sins and evil deeds, and by performing righteous good deeds), and is patient, then surely, Allah makes not the reward of the Muhsinun (good-doers) to be lost."

Allah(سبحانه وتعلى) says about Luqmân:

﴿يَا بُنَيَّ أَقِمِ الصَّلَاةَ وَأْمُرْ بِالْمَعْرُوفِ وَانْهَ عَنِ الْمُنكَرِ وَاصْبِرْ عَلَى مَا أَصَابَكَ إِنَّ ذَلِكَ مِنْ عَزْمِ الْأُمُورِ﴾[318]

"O my son! Aqim-is-Salat (perform As-Salat), enjoin (people) for Al-Ma'ruf (Islamic Monotheism and all that is good), and forbid (people) from Al-Munkar (i.e. disbelief in the Oneness of Allah, polytheism of all kinds and all that is evil and bad), and bear with patience whatever befall you. Verily! These are some of the important commandments ordered by Allah with no exemption."

Allah(سبحانه وتعلى) says:

﴿...وَبَشِّرِ الصَّابِرِينَ﴾[319]

[316] Ali 'Imrân: 200
[317] Yoosuf: 90
[318] Luqman: 17

"And give glad tidings to As-Sabirin (the patient ones, etc.)."

In matters of obedience, the believer is commanded to be sincere and to seek forgiveness.

Allah(سبحانه وتعلى) says:

﴿فَاعْلَمْ أَنَّهُ لا إِلَهَ إِلاَّ اللَّهُ وَاسْتَغْفِرْ لِذَنبِكَ وَلِلْمُؤْمِنِينَ وَالْمُؤْمِنَاتِ﴾[320]

"So know (O Muhammad) that none has the right to be worshipped but Allah, and ask forgiveness for your sin, and also for (the sin of) believing men and believing women."

Allah(سبحانه وتعلى) says:

﴿أَلاَّ تَعْبُدُواْ إِلاَّ اللَّهَ إِنَّنِي لَكُم مِّنْهُ نَذِيرٌ وَبَشِيرٌ * وَأَنِ اسْتَغْفِرُواْ رَبَّكُمْ ثُمَّ تُوبُواْ إِلَيْهِ...﴾[321]

"(Saying) worship none but Allah. Verily, I (Muhammad) am unto you from Him a warner and a bringer of glad tidings. And (commanding you): 'Seek the forgiveness of your Lord, and turn to Him in repentance.'"

Allah(سبحانه وتعلى) says:

﴿قُلْ إِنَّمَا أَنَا بَشَرٌ مِّثْلُكُمْ يُوحَى إِلَيَّ أَنَّمَا إِلَهُكُمْ إِلَهٌ وَاحِدٌ فَاسْتَقِيمُوا إِلَيْهِ وَاسْتَغْفِرُوهُ...﴾[322]

"Say (O Muhammad): "I am only a human being like you. It is inspired in me that your Ilah (God) is One Ilah (God - Allah), therefore take Straight Path to Him (with true Faith Islamic Monotheism) and obedience to Him, and seek forgiveness of Him."

[319] Al-Baqarah: 155
[320] Muhammad: 19
[321] Hood: 2-3
[322] Fussilat:6

The Prophet ﷺ has said: "O people! Repent before your Lord, because I repent to Him hundred times a day. Moreover, he ﷺ has said: "There is (at times) some sort of shade upon my heart, and I seek forgiveness from Allah hundred times a day." These two Hadith have been reported by Imam Muslim.[323]

It is narrated by al-Bukhari, on the authority of Abu Hurayrah ﷺ that the Messenger of Allah ﷺ has said: "By the name of Allah, I seek forgiveness and repent before Him more than seventy times in a day".[324]

Summary of this: Every action has two principles; likewise, the Qadar must also have two principles.

The Two Principles of Action:

I. A principle preceding the action or whatever is similar to it. It is striving to implement it in knowledge and action. Thus, a person will strive to [attain] knowledge about Allah(سبحانه وتعلى), His Names, Attributes and His laws, then he will act according to that knowledge by affirming the information or by enacting the laws, thereby fulfilling the commandments and avoid the prohibitions.

II. A principle following that action. It is seeking forgiveness or repentance from any shortcomings in enacting the commands or in avoiding the forbidden. That is why it is recommended to conclude the action by seeking forgiveness, as Allah(سبحانه وتعلى) says:

﴿...وَالْمُسْتَغْفِرِينَ بِالأَسْحَارِ﴾[325]

[323] Muslim. The Book of remembrance Allah ﷻ, Chapter: the Virtue of Remembering Allah ﷻ...

[324] Al-Bukhari

[325] Ali 'Imran: 17

"Those who pray and beg Allah's Pardon in the last hours of the night."

The companions of Prophet ﷺ used to pray at night and conclude it with seeking of forgiveness. Prophet ﷺ used to do seek forgiveness thrice (three times) upon completing his prayer.[326] Moreover, the last surah that was revealed to him was an-Nasr:

﴿إِذَا جَاءَ نَصْرُ اللَّهِ وَالْفَتْحُ * وَرَأَيْتَ النَّاسَ يَدْخُلُونَ فِي دِينِ اللَّهِ أَفْوَاجًا * فَسَبِّحْ بِحَمْدِ رَبِّكَ وَاسْتَغْفِرْهُ إِنَّهُ كَانَ تَوَّابًا﴾[327]

"When comes the Help of Allah (to you, O Muhammad against your enemies) and the conquest (of Makkah), And you see that the people enter Allah's religion (Islam) in crowds, So glorify the Praises of your Lord, and ask for His Forgiveness. Verily, He is the One Who accepts the repentance and forgives."

After the revelation of this surah, Prophet ﷺ would increasingly recite: سُبْحَانَكَ اللَّهُمَّ رَبَّنَا وَبِحَمْدِكَ اللَّهُمَّ اغْفِرْلِيْ [How perfect You are, Our Lord, and I praise You, and I ask Your forgiveness] in his Ruku' and Sujud. Additionally, its revelation was a sign of the impending death of the Prophet ﷺ. It has been narrated by Ibn 'Abbas ؓ in the gathering of the Commander of the Faithful, 'Umar ibn al-Khattâb ؓ, and other companions, and Umar has approved of it while saying: "I do not know about it other than what you said."[328]

In Sahih Muslim, it is reported by Aishah ؓ that she has said: Before he ﷺ died, the Prophet ﷺ used to recite more often:

سُبْحَانَكَ وَبِحَمْدِكَ وَ أَسْتَغْفِرُكَ وَأَتُوْبُ إِلَيْكَ

---

[326] Muslim
[327] An-Nasr (110)
[328] Al-Bukhari (3672)

(How perfect You are, and I praise You, and I ask Your pardon, and turn in repentance to You)." Thus, he has made Tawbah and Istighfâr the last actions of his life.

Two Principles of Qadar:

First Principle: Before the pre-destined event takes place, one must seek assistance and refuge from Allah(سبحانه وتعلى), and beseech Him, out of hope and fear; thus, he would be fully reliant on his Lord, turning to Him for achieving the good or for keeping away from the evil.

Second Principle: After the event takes place, one is to be patient upon his destiny, whether for missing the desire or for the occurrence of misfortune. He should console himself by acknowledging that whatever befalls him, it could not have been avoided, and whatever does not happen to him, nothing could have made it happen. Moreover, he should acknowledge that the situation cannot be altered from what it has been destined for. He should be pleased with his situation and conformed to it. There should not be any kind of regret or sadness about it.

As Allah(سبحانه وتعلى) says:

﴿مَا أَصَابَ مِن مُّصِيبَةٍ إِلاَّ بِإِذْنِ اللَّهِ وَمَن يُؤْمِن بِاللَّهِ يَهْدِ قَلْبَهُ وَاللَّهُ بِكُلِّ شَيْءٍ عَلِيمٌ﴾[329]

"No calamity befalls, but with the Leave [i.e. decision and Qadar (Divine Preordainments)] of Allah, and whosoever believes in Allah, He guides his heart [to the true Faith with certainty, i.e. what has befallen him was already written for him by Allah from the Qadar (Divine Preordainments)], and Allah is the All-Knower of everything."

Ibn 'Abbâs ﷺ says that "He guides his heart" means that He guides his heart towards firm belief in that whatever befalls him, it could not have

[329] At-Taghabun: 11

been avoided, and whatever does not happen to him, nothing could have made it happen.

'Alqamah, in the interpretation of this verse, says: "He is a person when any misfortune befalls him, he realizes it is from Allah so he becomes pleased and submits".

Therefore, whoever follows these guidelines –as we have explained previously– for any action or qadar, then he is a righteous slave of Allah(سبحانه وتعلى), who seeks assistance from Allah(سبحانه وتعلى) while relying on Him. He is among the people whom Allah(سبحانه وتعلى) has blessed. Allah(سبحانه وتعلى) mentions these two principles together in more than one place.

As Allah(سبحانه وتعلى) says:

﴿إِيَّاكَ نَعْبُدُ وَإِيَّاكَ نَسْتَعِينُ﴾[330]

"You (Alone) we worship, and You (Alone) we ask for help (for each and everything)."

And Allah(سبحانه وتعلى) says:

﴿...فَاعْبُدْهُ وَتَوَكَّلْ عَلَيْهِ ...﴾[331]

"So worship Him (O Muhammad) and put your trust in Him."

And Allah(سبحانه وتعلى) says:

﴿...وَمَا تَوْفِيقِي إِلاَّ بِاللَّهِ عَلَيْهِ تَوَكَّلْتُ وَإِلَيْهِ أُنِيبُ﴾[332]

"And my guidance cannot come except Allah, in Him I trust and unto Him, I repent."

[330] Al-Fâtihah: 5
[331] Hood: 123
[332] Ibid: 88

People regarding Shari'ah and Qadr

People – regarding Shari'ah [legislated actions] and Qadr – are divided into four groups:

- They who implement these four principles: The two principles of legislated actions [Shari'ah] and the two principles of Qadr. These are the true believers and God-fearing people, who have a sufficient share of devotion to Allah(سبحانه وتعلى) and seeking His help to set aright their affairs. They live for the sake of Allah(سبحانه وتعلى), in a state of devotion to Allah(سبحانه وتعلى). They are the people of moderation and integrity who realize the true station of [Allah(سبحانه وتعلى)'s] Rububiyah [Lordship] and Uluhiyah [Divinity]. This is the noblest of the groups. Indeed, this is the status of those that Allah(سبحانه وتعلى) has blessed, among the prophets, the truthful, the martyrs, and the righteous.
- They who fall short in implementing the principles of Qadar. They have a sufficient share of devotion to Allah(سبحانه وتعلى) and steadfastness upon His legislation; yet, they do not adequately seek the help of Allah(سبحانه وتعلى) nor remain patient upon His universal and legislative decrees. Thus, they are unable to tolerate the difficulties – a sense of weakness and laziness overcomes them, which hinders them from accomplishing or continuing the action. Additionally, after performing the action, they are overcome with a sense of arrogance and pride, which may result in nullifying their actions or their humiliation. This group holds a lower status than the previous group because their fulfillment of the station of Uluhiyah [Divinity] is stronger than the station of Rububiyah [Lordship].
- They who fall short in implementing the principles of legislated actions. They are weak in their steadfastness upon the commands of Allah(سبحانه وتعلى) and adherence to His

legislation; yet, they are strong in seeking assistance from Allah(سبحانه وتعلى) and reliance on Him. However, this reliance can sometimes be in matters that are disliked by

Allah(سبحانه وتعلى).

Thus, he may be helped or enabled according to his needs, and doors may be opened for him that would not have happened for the previous group. Nevertheless, whatever he achieves is in the worldly matters, and there is nothing for him in the hereafter except misery. This is because he is not God-fearing; indeed, the [goodly] hereafter is only for the God-fearing people.

As Allah(سبحانه وتعلى) says:

﴿فَإِذَا رَكِبُوا فِي الْفُلْكِ دَعَوُا اللَّهَ مُخْلِصِينَ لَهُ الدِّينَ فَلَمَّا نَجَّاهُمْ إِلَى الْبَرِّ إِذَا هُمْ يُشْرِكُونَ * لِيَكْفُرُوا بِمَا آتَيْنَاهُمْ وَلِيَتَمَتَّعُوا فَسَوْفَ يَعْلَمُونَ﴾[333]

"And when they embark on a ship, they invoke Allah, making their Faith pure for Him only, but when He brings them safely to land, behold, they give a share of their worship to others. So that they become ingrate for that which We have given them, and that they take their enjoyment (as a warning and a threat), but they will come to know."

Indeed, Allah(سبحانه وتعلى) knows that they will associate partners with Him after He rescues them. However, when they are in the sea, they are sincere and truthful in their prayer for rescue, so Allah(سبحانه وتعلى) granted their prayer. However, due to their lack of steadfastness upon worship, they lose the rewards in the hereafter.

The difference between this group and the previous one: The previous group is weak because of their weak reliance and seeking assistance from Allah(سبحانه وتعلى); however, they remain steadfast upon [the action], as

[333] Al-'Ankaboot: 65-66

long as they are not hindered by weakness and laziness. On the other hand, although this group has a strong [reliance], it does not benefit them unless they conform to the commands and follow the Sunnah.

- They who fall short in implementing the principles of legislated actions and the principles of Qadr. They neither worship nor seek assistance from Allah(سبحانه وتعلى) or rely on Him at times of difficulty; rather, they are arrogant to perform acts of worship, thinking themselves self-sufficient. Sometimes, they may seek refuge at times of difficulties in Satan; thus, they worship [Satan] according to his wish, and Satan helps them in what they want. Some people may [wrongfully] think that this [being secure at times of difficulty by the help of Satan] is a sign of honor and privilege; rather, it is a sign of humiliation. Indeed, they will reap the evil and humiliating consequences in the hereafter for what they have done. This is the worst group among the above groups.

Differentiation and Comparison among People of Innovation

Observers among the philosophers, who claim themselves as practicing Muslims and followers of the Sunnah, believe that Tawheed is fulfilling Tawheed ar-Rububiyah only.

The Sufi groups, who claim themselves as practicing Muslims and more knowledgeable, believe that the purpose of Tawheed is achieving Tawheed ar-Rububiyah. It is known that this purpose of Tawheed has been acknowledged by the Mushrikeen. Moreover, it is not sufficient to make a person Muslim, let alone be a close friend of Allah(سبحانه وتعلى) or from the best of them.

Another group also agrees with this meaning of Tawheed; however, they add to that the negation of the attributes of Allah(سبحانه وتعالى). In doing so, they ascribe deficiencies and fall in the error of suspension. They are even worse than many Mushrikeen.

Jahm bin Safwân, the Imâm of the Jahmiyah – those who negate the attributes – transgresses in matters of Qada' [Devine Decree] and Qadar [Predestination] and beliefs in determinism [جبر]. His view in this issue is similar with the view of polytheists who say, "If Allah(سبحانه وتعالى) had willed, we would not have taken partners [in worship] with Him, nor would our fathers, and we would not have forbidden anything [against His Will]." Nevertheless, he affirms the commands and prohibitions, thereby differing from the Mushrikeen. However, he believes in [excessive] hope. In doing so, he lightens the issue of commands, prohibitions, and punishments, because according to him the one who commits major sins is a perfect believer and is not deserving of punishment.

Najjâriyyah – the followers of Husain bin Muhammad al-Najjar – and the Dharariyah – the followers of Dharar bin 'Amr and Hafs al-Fard – are similar to the Jahmiyah in the matters of Qada', Eemân, and the negation of attributes.

Kilâbiyah – the followers of 'Abdullah bin Sa'eed bin Kilâb – and al-Ash'ariyah – who follow Abu al-Hasan al-Ash'ari – are better than the previous groups in the issue of Attributes. They affirm Rational Attributes[334] [الصفات العقلية] and their leaders affirm Informational Attributes[335] [الصفات الخبرية] in general. As for the issues of Qadar, Names, and legislation, the opinions of all of these groups are very similar.

---

[334] Rational Attributes are those that can be deduced by the intellect.

[335] Informational Attributes are those that are expressly stated in the Qur'an or Sunnah.

In these two issues, however, the followers of ibn Kilâb, such as al-Hârith al-Muhâsibi, are better than the Ash'ariyah.

Al-Karrâmiyah – the followers of Muhammad bin Karâm – have similar views in the issues of Attributes, Qadar, and promises of reward and punishment to most of the philosophers, whose statements are in clear opposition to the Sunnah. However, their views about Eemân is invalid; indeed, nobody has ever stated anything like them before. According to them, Eemân is only testifying through the tongue, even if it is without approval by the heart; thus, according to them, a hypocrite is considered a believer, yet he will abide in the Hellfire forever.

Mu'tazilah – the followers of Wâsil bin 'Atâ', who has isolated himself from the gatherings of Hasan al-Basri – have similar views on the attributes like the Jahmiyah; they negate the Attributes. Nevertheless, they differ from them in the issues of Qadar, Names and legislation. In the issues of Qadar, they believe that the slave is independent in his actions and choices, whereupon Allah(سبحانه وتعلى) neither predefines his actions nor creates them. Therefore, it is a kind of Shirk in this aspect.

On the other hand, Jahm says that the slave is compelled to do his action; he has no choice in it.

In the issues of Names and legislations, Mu'tazilah says: committing major sin expels a person from the circle of Eemân but it will not bring him within the boundary of disbelief, rather, he is in between two positions. Nevertheless, he will abide in the Hellfire forever. On the other hand, Jahm says the man has full Eemân and is not deserving of entering the hellfire.

As per the issues of Qadar, Names and legislation, the Mu'tazilah are better than the Jahmiyah, because affirming the commandments, prohibitions, and promises of reward and punishment while negating the Qadar is better than affirming the Qadar while denying the commandments, prohibitions and promises of reward and punishment. Therefore, during the companions of Prophet's time, no one has ever denied the commandments, prohibitions, and promises of reward and punishment; yet, there have been people during that time who belong to al-Qadariyah, al-Khawârij and al-Harooriyyah.

Indeed, it is natural that the light innovations occur first, and whenever the knowledgeable people, those who are guided with the Prophetic light, become weak, the innovations become stronger. And the closer to the era of the Salaf and the Imâm(s) a person is, the more preferable and stronger his opinions are.

The Sufi groups, those who propagate the universal truth [الحقيقة الكونية] while neglecting the commandments and prohibitions, are worse than the al-Qadariyah al-Mu'tazilah and their likes. Because these Sufi groups are similar in their opinion to those Mushrikeen who say,

﴿...لَوْ شَاءَ اللَّهُ مَا أَشْرَكْنَا...﴾[336]

"If Allah had willed, we would not have taken partners (in worship) with Him."

Moreover, al-Qadariyah is similar to those pagans who believe that there are two creators for the universe, and the Mushrikeen are worse than the pagans.

And the Sufi groups who respect the commandments and prohibitions while preferring Tawheed ar-Rububiyah and affirming al-Qadar are better than the Mu'tazilah. However, they are similar to the Mu'tazilah from another perspective; they consider the objective of Tawheed as achieving Tawheed ar-Rububiyah and transcending to it. In doing so, they isolate themselves from the real Muslim community and from their

[336] Al-An'am: 148

methodology. Indeed, whatever they have innovated may even be worse than the innovation of those Mu'tazilah.

The misguidance and innovation of all of these groups are proportional to their differing from the Muslim community and from their methodology. The religion of Allah(سبحانه وتعلى) is what has been brought by His messengers and what the Books have been sent with. This is the Straight Path, the Path of the Prophet ﷺ and his companions, the best generation among the nations.

Allah(سبحانه وتعلى) has commanded us to say in our prayer:

﴿اهدِنَا الصِّرَاطَ الْمُسْتَقِيمَ * صِرَاطَ الَّذِينَ أَنْعَمْتَ عَلَيْهِمْ غَيْرِ الْمَغْضُوبِ عَلَيْهِمْ وَلاَ الضَّالِّينَ﴾[337]

"Guide us to the Straight Way. The Way of those on whom You have bestowed Your Grace, not (the way) of those who earned Your Anger (such as the Jews), nor of those who went astray (such as the Christians)."

Here, ﴿الْمَغْضُوبِ عَلَيْهِمْ﴾ refers to the Jews, who know the right path but do not follow it, and ﴿الضَّالِّينَ﴾ refers to the Christians, who worship Allah(سبحانه وتعلى) without knowledge. It has been said: Seek refuge in Allah(سبحانه وتعلى) from the tribulation of the sinful scholar and from the ignorant worshiper. 'Abdullah ibn Mas'ud ﷺ says: the Prophet ﷺ drew a line for us, then he said, "This is the straight path of Allah." Then he drew some lines to the left and right sides of it, and said, "Upon each of these lines [paths] is a devil who invites people towards him." Then, the Prophet ﷺ recited the following verse:

﴿وَأَنَّ هَذَا صِرَاطِي مُسْتَقِيمًا فَاتَّبِعُوهُ وَلاَ تَتَّبِعُواْ السُّبُلَ فَتَفَرَّقَ بِكُمْ عَن سَبِيلِهِ ذَلِكُمْ وَصَّاكُم بِهِ لَعَلَّكُمْ تَتَّقُونَ﴾[338]

[337] Al-Fatiha: 6-7

"And verily, this (i.e. Allah's Commandments) is my Straight Path, so follow it, and follow not (other) paths, for they will separate you away from His Path. This He has ordained for you that you may become Al-Muttaqun."

Hudhayfah bin al-Yamân ﷺ says: "O group of al-Qurra![339] Follow the straight path, and choose the path of those people who were before you, for then you would have taken a great lead [and will be the leaders], but if you divert right or left, then you will go astray far away."[340]

'Abdullah bin Mas'ud ﷺ says: "Whoever among you wants to follow the Sunnah, he should follow those who have passed away because the one who is alive is not secure from the Fitnah [tribulations]. They are the Companions of Muhammad ﷺ. They are the best among his Ummah, the purest in heart, the deepest in knowledge, and the farthest from the false display of piety. They are a community whom God chose for the company of His Prophet ﷺ and the establishment of His religion. Therefore, acknowledge their rightful status, follow their paths; indeed, they are upon the true guidance."

We pray to Almighty Allah(سبحانه وتعلى) that He includes us among these righteous people, and deviates not our hearts [from the truth] after He has guided us.

All praise and thanks be to Allah(سبحانه وتعلى), Lord of the worlds [mankind, Jinn and all that exists]. (Completed on 22/05/1410 A.H)

---

[338] Al-An'am: 153

[339] Al-Qurrâ': Religious scholars in the knowledge of the Qur'an and Sunnah or those who know the Qur'an by heart.

[340] Al-Bukhari: The Book of Holding fast to the Qur'an and the *Sunnah*; Chapter: Following the *Sunnah* (Legal ways of the Prophet).

Glossary

Ahl Badr: Those sahâba who joined the battle of Badr, which is the first great battle in Islamic history.
Al-Hulool: Incarnation; Immanentism; Pantheism; belief in the immanence of God.
Al-Ahkâm: Islamic Rules and regulations.

Asma' Allah: Names of Allah سبحانه وتعالى

Al-Hayyiz: Deeming something to occupy a particular place.
Al-Khawarij: An early sect in Islamic History, who believe that major sins take one out of Islam. They came to be called the Khawarij – "the Seceders" or "the Rebels" – because of their khuruj (rebellion) against 'Ali ibn Abi Talib رضي الله عنه.
Al-Lawhu al-Mahfuj: The Preserved Tablet.
Al-Mawjud al-Mumkin / al-wujud al-mumkin: The contingent existence, this defines the existence of created things that may or may not exist. Created things have no independent being and their existence is not necessary. Allah (سبحانه وتعالى) Most High brought them into being through His will, power and knowledge and if He willed, they would have no existence.
Al-Qadar: The fate, the destiny, divine preordainment.
Al-Qadariyah: One of the earliest misguided groups in Islamic history. They believe that the person is independent in doing his actions by his power and will and Allah(سبحانه وتعالى) has nothing to do with his action.
Al-Râfidah: The term is used by Sunni Muslims to refer to the Shiites who do not recognize Abu Bakr and his successors as

legitimate rulers of the Muslim nation and revolted against Zayd Ibn 'Ali's tyranny.
At-Ta'teel: Suspending God of all attributes; the opposite of at-Tashbeeh.
Al-Ta'weel: Some scholars consider ta'wil to mean foregoing the literal meaning of a text for its metaphorical sense without violating the norms of Arabic language for metaphorical usage, and in consonance with metaphorical relations.
At-Tafweed: Leaving the verses related to the Attributes of Allah(سبحانه وتعالى) without trying to understand them.
Tahayyuz: The Tahayyuz of Allah(سبحانه وتعالى) refers to Him occupying a certain location.
At-Tahreef: Corruption of a text, it also refers to false interpretation.
At-Tamtheel: Resembling any of Allah(سبحانه وتعالى)'s attributes with His creations; likening these attributes to those of His creation.
At-Tashbeeh: likening of any of Allah(سبحانه وتعالى)'s attributes to anything else.
At-Tazâhum:Crowding; namely that of Allah(سبحانه وتعالى)'s attributes.
Al-Wa'd: The promise made by Allah(سبحانه وتعالى) to the slaves that, if they obey Allah (سبحانه وتعالى)'s commands they will be rewarded.
Al-Wa'eed: The warning made by Allah(سبحانه وتعالى) to the human being that, if they disobey Him, He will punish them.
A'râd: Something nonessential; which can be displayed or appear only through the body.

Athar: The saying of the Prophet's companions.
Bid'ah: Bid'ah in religious terms is referred to as anything which was not sanctioned by Muhammad ﷺ or his Sahâba ﷺ.
Hajj: One of the five pillars of Islam is pilgrimage that occurs during the Islamic month of Dhu al-Hijjah to the holy city of Makkah.
Ijma': Consensus; an opinion agreed upon between all Muslim scholars.
Imâmah: Imâmah is the Shia doctrine of the religious, spiritual and political leadership of the Ummah. The Shia believe that the A'immah – "Imams" – are the true caliphs or rightful successors of Muhammad, and some of them further that Imams possess the supernatural knowledge, authority, and 'Ismah – "infallibility" – as well as being part of the Ahl al-Bayt. The family of Prophet Muhammad ﷺ.
Imâms: The Islamic religious leaders, especially those famous Imâms like Abu Hanifa, Shafi, Malik and Ahmad bin Hanbal.
Khalaf: The generation after the sahâba and tâbi'een, some of which innovated many things after the golden era.
Khilâfah: It refers to the first system of government established in Islam, and represented the political unity of the Muslim Ummah "Nation".
Mubtadi': innovator; who practices or advocates bid'ah.
Muhkam: Muhkam verses contain definite teachings of the Qur'an and are explicitly clear in their understanding.
Musalli: A person who performs salâh (prayer).
Mumaththil: Mushabbih; People who resemble Allah(سبحانه وتعالى) with His creatures.
Mumtani' al-Wajood: That which cannot exist.
Murji'ah: Who proclaimed "No Kufr, except the Kufr of Juhood (rejection) and Takdheeb (denial)." A sinner, according to them, is considered a perfect believer no matter what sins he commits

or what duties he fails to perform since they also deny that Emân increases and decreases.

Mushabbih: Mumaththil; People who resemble Allah(سبحانه وتعالى) with His creatures.

Mutahayyiz: That which occupies a particular place or location.

Mutashâbih: Mutashâbih verse contains meaning that can be unclear to the general people.

Nooniyyah: This is the title of a famous poem, written by Ibn al-Qayyim, all the verses of which end with the letter Noon.

Sahâba: The companions of the Prophet Muhammad ﷺ.

Saheehayn: The two sources of Hadith; Namely Bukhari and Muslim.

Rububiyyah: Oneness of Lordship, the admission that Allah(سبحانه وتعالى) alone is the Creator of everything.

Salaf: The righteous people of the Islamic golden era.

Sutra: Something which is placed in front of a person while praying, to indicate to others that they should not cross between the Musalli and the sutra.

Tâbi'een: The generation of Muslims who were born after the death of the Prophet Muhammad ﷺ, but who were contemporaries of the Sahâba.

Ta'teel: See at-Ta'teel.

Tahreef: See at-Tahreef.

Tajseem: Describing Allah(سبحانه وتعالى) as having a body.

Tamtheel: See at-Tamtheel.

Takyeef: Explaining the "kayf" (how) about Allah(سبحانه وتعالى) without any evidence. For example, to explain how He is sitting, how His hand is, or how His eyes are.

Uluhiyyah: Oneness of Worship of Allah(سبحانه وتعالى), the fact that He deserves to be worshipped Alone without any partner.
Ummah: In the context of Islam, the word ummah is used to mean the diaspora or "Community of the Believers" (ummat al-mu'mineen), and thus the whole Muslim world.
Wâjib al-wujood: The necessarily existent, which defines the existence of Allah(سبحانه وتعالى).
He exists independently through Himself and His existence is necessary for the existence of all other things.
Zakah: One of the five pillars of Islam. It is the giving of 2.5% of one's possessions to charity, generally to the poor and needy.

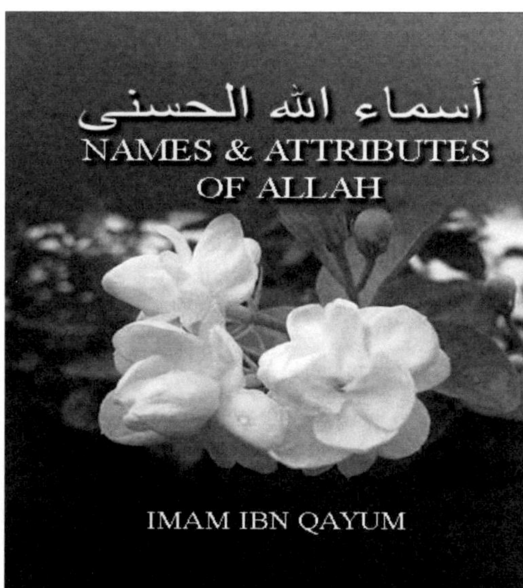

Forthcoming Book from Al-Naseehah Pubs